A Glimpse of Heaven

The Remarkable World of
Spiritually Transformative Experiences

D1466719

Adams Media
Avon, Massachusetts

Published by
Adams Media, an F+W Publications Company
57 Littlefield Street, Avon, MA 02322. U.S.A.
www.adamsmedia.com

ISBN: 1-58062-947-4

Printed in the United States of America.

J I H G F E D C B A

Library of Congress Cataloging-in-Publication Data
Wills-Brandon, Carla
A glimpse of heaven / Carla Wills-Brandon.
p.   cm.
Includes bibliographical references
ISBN 1-58062-947-4
1. Parapsychology. 2. Spiritual life—Miscellanea. I. Title.
BF1031.W68 2003
133.9—dc21
2003004477

This publication is designed to provide accurate and authoritative information with
regard to the subject matter covered. It is sold with the understanding that the
publisher is not engaged in rendering legal, accounting, or other professional advice.
If legal advice or other expert assistance is required, the services of a competent
professional person should be sought.
　　—From a *Declaration of Principles* jointly adopted by a Committee of the
American Bar Association and a Committee of Publishers and Associations

Many of the designations used by manufacturers and sellers to distinguish their
products are claimed as trademarks. Where those designations appear in this
book and Adams Media was aware of a trademark claim, the designations have
been printed in initial capital letters.

Cover illustration by © Vicky Emptage / Getty Images.

This book is available at quantity discounts for bulk purchases.
For information, call 1-800-872-5627.

Angels Come A-Tumbling

Angels come a-tumbling through a tunnel of light.
With open arms they gently embrace our Dear Ones,
offering a fantastic ride to the Other Side.
For us, this is not the final
"Goodbye."
When we go to sleep, Dear Ones return to our side.
Bringing Love from Above,
they tumble into our dreams each night.

Dedication

This book is dedicated to my soul mate,
Michael

To the two angels in my life,
Aaron and Joshua

And to my mother-in-law,
Dr. Elizabeth Brandon,
Who is finally flying high with my father-in-law,
Dr. Sylvan Brandon

Acknowledgments

*W*riting a book is always a spiritual adventure. Words flow from a higher-powered source, and I'm always amazed at what ends up on paper. Loving hands then polish my messy text and the final message is finally put forth for all to enjoy. There is a flow to the craft of book writing, but with this tenth project, that flow was briefly interrupted. When my mother-in-law passed, my family and I were with her. As she made the journey from this life to the next, we received a brief glimpse of heaven. Once I returned to the task of completing this book, I found the words flowed even more smoothly. Thank you, Mom. Your final gift will forever be treasured.

Many thanks also go out to my agent and good friend, John White, who soothes my ruffled feathers on a regular basis. Also, I must express my admiration for Claire Gurus. She encouraged me to go ahead with this project, which eventually landed in the lap of a talented and very patient editor named Danielle Chiotti. Great polish job, "Daniella!" And thanks to wonderful copyeditors, Laura MacLaughlin and Andrea Mattei, this book really shines. It is also extremely important to note that if those who contributed to this book had not courageously stepped forward, this undertaking would never have been possible.

Finally, I must share that my family has traveled down many "manuscript" roads with me. I know this one was particularly personal, as it was written while "Grandma" crossed over. Know that I love you, Michael, Aaron, and Joshua.

Contents

You Are Not Alone

The fruits of spiritual travel
are rich with adventure.
A vivid assortment of color awaits you.
Spectacular sensations linger just beyond the veil of
    the unknown,
to vitalize not only what you see, hear, taste, and smell,
but also to awaken those sleeping senses,
senses which have yet to be recognized.
With the "aw" of a child,
take the plunge and know that we will be with you,
to guide you and teach you.

Foreword

$\mathcal{S}$ everal years ago, a patient of mine died a tragic death. This young teen was incredibly bright, had conquered a battle with drug addiction, and was just beginning what should have been the rest of a very productive life. Sadly, a violent accident put an end to this. As one can imagine, the family was devastated.

After the funeral, the mother, father, and younger brother returned to my office to begin the long, drawn-out healing process of grieving. Through the tears and rage, the family made progress, but still felt the deep sense of emptiness that often accompanies such a loss.

During one session, the mother asked, "Do you know who George Anderson is?" I replied, "No, can't say I've ever heard of him." She then looked at me hard and long as if pondering whether or not to continue this discussion. "He's a medium," she announced. In my ignorance, I asked, "What's a medium? Is that like a psychic?" Defensively, she replied, "No, a medium is different than a psychic. A true medium is someone who can make contact with those living in the afterlife." With the raise of an eyebrow, I replied, "Oh, really? There's a difference?" Smiling at my obvious lack of awareness, she then added, "I'm thinking about making an appointment with him. What's your opinion?"

Upon hearing this, the scientist in me, who had spent several years researching those childhood variables predicting difficulty in school, utilizing a complicated statistical analysis, just smiled back and said, "Well, if you think this will help you, if you think this Anderson person is credible, check into it. In the meantime, let me ask my wife what she knows about him."

My wife, who I often refer to as eccentric and, at times, "Ms. Spooky" for her investigations into unusual occurrences with death and dying, along with afterlife experiences, just happened to be in the office next door. As I made notes about my patient's decision to contact George Anderson, I also made a mental note to catch Carla between patients and razz her about this medium, or as I used to say so often, "one of her kind."

Sitting at the kitchen table of our 100-year-old office house, I asked Carla, "Who is this George Anderson?" Immediately, her eyes lit up. With this I thought, "Oh, no. There's that look. Here we go again with another lecture on the overwhelming evidence supporting an afterlife existence." Grabbing her lunch, which in my opinion was as curious as her afterlife beliefs, she sat down and said, "George Anderson? Now just where would someone like you hear his name?"

While I chugged a soda and munched on peanuts, out came the barbeque tofu and the soymilk. Taking a big bite of tofu, my wife announced, "George Anderson is a famous American medium and author. He's reached celebrity status but I wouldn't think someone like yourself would have a clue about him." As we had our lunch, I explained to her the conversation which had transpired in my office, just minutes ago. "I'm all for it," she said. I smiled and replied, "I knew you would be."

My clients received an incredible reading from medium George Anderson. He passed on to them things about their deceased loved one that could only have come from the young teen. As these parents shared their experience with me, I found I was speechless. I had successfully aided this family in connecting with their grief. With therapeutic measures, I had intervened on self-destructive behavior with the remaining son.

In spite of my ability, I could never give them back their oldest child. Thankfully, a medium had been able to do what I could not. He completed the task by providing this grieving family with a direct connection to their departed child. I found the transformation not only healing, but also amazing. Though my own wife had been investigating spiritually transformative experiences for over a decade, she could not be my teacher. I had to learn this lesson from my own patients, and for such a lesson, I will always be grateful.

Since that time, my skepticism of experiences of this nature, encounters yet to be completely measured and explained with concrete statistics, has lessened. As luck would have it, I too eventually came face to face with not only departing visions, but also an after-death communication. As the death of my own father drew near, I witnessed "something" leaving his body. A swirl of misty pastel color escaped his chest area. Hard as I tried, I could find no logical explanation for this. After he died in my arms, my own grief overwhelmed me, but an after-death vision of him soothed my pain. The day after his death, I visually saw him, looking whole and well, sitting in our downstairs parlor on the couch. This was my glimpse of heaven.

After these experiences, I was cautious about openly sharing them. I was a scientifically minded, meat and potatoes, male mental health professional, who trusted only black-and-white statistics, born and raised in Texas by a logically minded university professor mother and atheist surgeon father. Despite my ingrained "after death you turn to worm food" upbringing, I had encountered several powerful spiritually transformative experiences within a relatively short period of time, and this had turned my once-predictable world upside down.

These encounters created a great deal of confusion for me, and for sometime after this, I could not incorporate them into my everyday living experience. Departing visions from the dying and communications from the deceased didn't fit in neatly with my very rigid frame of mind. I needed another form of "grounding" to come to terms with what I had experienced, and for this, I turned to my wife, Carla, the author of the book you are about to read.

Contained within the following pages is an exciting message. The message is: There is more to life than meets the eye. Today, even *I* believe this message. The first part of this message is that the unexplained cannot easily be dismissed with current-day medical, psychological, or scientific thinking.

There is a second part to this message that assures us that these experiences are not uncommon or unusual. This point was proven to me after Carla released her last book, *One Last Hug Before I Go: The Mystery and Meaning of Deathbed Visions*. In response to this work, she received almost 2,000 additional after-death communications, near-death experiences, out of body adventures, departing visions, meditation moments of enlightenment, and precognitive experiences.

Though each account is unique to the experiencer, they all have several common threads, one being that integrating these events into the everyday living experience is often difficult and, at times, a lonely pursuit. Our culture does not give experiencers permission to openly discuss such matters. Understanding how to incorporate these fantastic encounters, these visions of the unseen, contacts with the afterlife, premonitions of things to come into the everyday living experience is often a challenge.

This book provides some answers. My wife has put together a sort of travel guide for those who are still grappling with their own spiritually transformative experiences. Travel through the following pages and learn how everyday people, just like you, are encountering a multitude of wonderful experiences, which suggest that science has an awful lot to learn about the human mind, life after death, and life as we know it. Discover how you can use your own STEs not only to enrich your life but that of those around you. I hope you enjoy the journey. I sure have.

—Michael Brandon, Ph.D.
September 18, 2002

chapter one

A Thunderous Awakening: "Am I the Only One?"

Two roads diverged in a wood, and I—
I took the one less traveled by,
And that has made all the difference.

—Robert Frost (1874–1963), from "The Road Not Taken," 1916

*F*or many years, I occupied a very lonely, hidden space on the peripheral edges of society. I felt as though I was on the outside looking in, isolated and unique. My perception of myself was very different from what the public saw. Privately, I believed I was an oddity, someone not quite glued together, and God forbid anyone should find out. Getting a glimpse of heaven, communicating with people who were supposed to be dead, waking up in a cold, hard sweat after another full-blown Technicolor dream, or predicting future events that inevitably came to pass were the norm for me. But I felt anything but normal.

At one time, encounters with the unusual or the unseen left me in a terrible state, feeling confused, frightened, and even embarrassed. To counter the fear, I closeted my numerous, often spontaneous, brushes with the spiritual away into the dark recesses of my psyche. There was the professional image to maintain. I was a well-respected published author and therapist, so in my mind, keeping that door locked tightly was a must.

These inexplicable spiritual encounters were not experiences to celebrate. If anything, for me these unplanned happenings felt like a curse. My early attempts at discussing such things with certain family members, friends, and professional peers, were typically met with ridicule, jokes, sarcasm, hurtful comments, suggestions of mental illness, and eye-rolling shame. The lack of support from those around me perpetuated a sense of alienation within me. It was a terrible emotional place in which to be. In order to survive, I eventually shut off access to my own marvelous spiritual adventures. I was afraid of what others would think, and the terror of being discovered was overwhelming.

Ultimately, this ever-mounting fear became the catalyst needed to unlock the chains barring entrance to this part of myself. Walking through my own door of fear and navigating many spiritual twists and turns was to become an amazing journey. In time, I would discover that my spiritual encounters were not only common, but normal human experiences. The trip from confusion and fear to wonderment and freedom began with a good-looking, fast-talking, energetic, unruly, chicory-drinking Cajun.

The Flicker of a Flame—a Beginning

The bayou carried water the color of milk chocolate through the local wetlands out to the sea. Because the water was so dark and full of silt, when fishing my sister had to tie the end of a silver spoon to a line to attract flounder, sea bass, and red fish to her hook. This might explain why the waterway was called Chocolate Bayou.

While consulting at a treatment facility on this bayou, I met up with another therapist who was a born-and-bred Cajun from Louisiana. He was full of good fun and we quickly became friends. Both of us put in long hours at this facility, and a periodic breath of fresh air provided a momentary chance to recharge. In between group therapy sessions and educational lectures, it was the habit of the staff to escape to the edge of the bayou. Under large trees full of gray Spanish moss, we would swap gossip and blow off steam. Eventually, the mosquitoes would outnumber us and we would retreat indoors, back to the hurting patients who so desperately needed our help.

During one break, my Cajun friend and I were sitting by the chocolate-colored bayou. He had been explaining to me how an old-style Louisiana pleasure, brewing the herb chicory with coffee, created a smooth cup of java. My friend had brought some of this Southern brew with him, and after offering me a sip he asked, "Why the down look? You aren't your usual perky self today. Crawdad got your tongue?"

After cracking a smile, I glanced up at him and replied, "I'm feeling a bit out of sync these days. Self-discovery isn't always a barrel of laughs." For months I had been revisiting my spiritual side. There was a crack in the door, but the pain and fear were once again becoming unbearable.

Sitting under a large, shady oak tree, swatting mosquitoes, I told my Cajun friend about the questions I had put before God. How do I deal with these periodic spiritual encounters? Was this normal, or was there something terribly wrong with me? I had worked so hard to clean up my old irresponsible, addictive behavior and heal the wounds of the past. Why was I still being visited by these spontaneous otherworldly experiences? They were in control of me and I was feeling totally out of control. As I asked each of these questions, large tears rolled down my face and a sense of hopelessness fell over me. At that moment, I felt as confused as the young addicts at the center, who were waiting inside for my words of wisdom. My dear friend then put his fragrant, sweet blend of chicory and coffee on the bank of the bayou and said, "Spiritually confused? I have a solution."

On that sultry, humid day by the bayou, as the flying fish jumped and the mosquitoes buzzed by, I learned how to meditate. My Cajun friend taught me how to use the flame of a lit candle to calm the jungle of thoughts and emotions streaming through my mind. From that moment on, I became dedicated to understanding the mysteries meditation had to offer me. I first began with the candle. Sitting on the floor, gazing into the light, I quickly discovered I could control the chatter in my head.

With this newfound focus, I started to glimpse another plane of existence, but this time, I felt in control. In this realm, I was introduced to my Higher Self, the true me. This Higher Self affirmed me, loved me, and guided me through another layer of childhood pain I had yet to address. It was a very healing time.

Eventually, I began to see the candles had only been a starting place. There was more to learn, and I knew it was time to move on. Though I had gained much insight, sitting quietly with my colorful candles, gazing into leaping flames, and exploring hand in hand with my Higher Self, my inner self, I had become curious about other methods of meditation.

A New Twist in the Road

After sipping chicory with my Cajun friend, I had also decided to start the next phase of my spiritual quest by taking a yoga class. One afternoon, my yoga instructor took a new turn in the road. "You don't know what Kundalini meditation is? You told me you had an out-of-body experience as a child. Didn't you know that's a byproduct of this form of yoga meditation? A spiritually progressed soul?" asked the petite woman wearing a white turban.

The room was packed, but the teacher was looking right at me, and I blushed from head to toe as I answered, "No." My first out-of-body adventure had been the result of a sexual trauma, not a moment of spiritual enlightenment. The instructor then began sharing with the class the philosophy behind Kundalini Yoga, also known as "The Yoga of Awareness." Though several students were very knowledgeable about Kundalini Yoga, it was news to me, and I felt like an idiot.

Sitting in a perfect Lotus position, cool as a cucumber, emanating enough spiritual energy to put the rest of us to shame, our instructor in the white turban enlightened the group: "According to archaeological digs in India, yoga has been around since 3000 B.C. Archaeologists have found numerous stones depicting images of various well-known yoga positions." Uncrossing her legs from the sitting Lotus position, our teacher clasped the bottoms of her feet and extended her legs outward, while bending at the waist. "Ouch!" I thought to myself. Being more than six feet tall and all legs, this new position was not for me. As she flexed her back and brought her chest to the floor, she ended her lecture: "Though there are several schools of yoga, Kundalini is one of the most powerful yoga disciplines."

After this particular yoga session, I began reading all I could on Kundalini Yoga. My short trek into the world of this ancient spiritual practice revealed that historical yogis, skilled in Kundalini meditation, were able to accomplish amazing feats such as levitation, fire walking, a sense of unity with the universe, spiritual bliss, and even astral projection (where the consciousness or soul separates from the body). After hearing all of this, I thought, "Gee, I could sure use a good dose of spiritual bliss!" What I also learned was that if done properly, Kundalini Yoga could awaken my untapped spiritual energy and explain some of my past unusual spiritual encounters.

So, out went my many multicolored candles with their dancing flames, and in came the typical Kundalini meditative visualization of a molten red, hot serpent of spiritual energy laying asleep at the base of my spine. Instead of focusing on the flickering light of a candle, my meditation sessions now involved a great deal more drama. Sitting comfortably in a Lotus position on the floor with my eyes closed, I would visualize the Kundalini serpent slithering up my spine in a coiling motion. Weaving its way through each of the visualized energy centers, or chakras, in my body, eventually the serpent would erupt into blue streams of light at the top of my head. I would then imagine this beautiful, powerful energy cascading down all sides of my perfectly still body. It was a lovely meditation, one that brought pure delight to my senses.

The "Crack"

One afternoon, I found myself seated on the floor with my legs crossed, preparing once again to dip into that well of spiritual glee, brought about by Kundalini meditation. Home alone, the silence of the house enveloped me like a warm, comforting blanket. Closing my eyes, I began visualizing the coiled energy at the base of my spine. Breathing deeply, I then used this air to push the visualized energy up my spine. In my mind's eye, the twisting and turning serpent made its way through my body, clearing out daily stress and tension.

All was going well, but unknown to me, on this particular day my meditation session would not end as usual. Outside, a typical Gulf Coast windstorm was beginning to die down, but a storm inside my soul was just beginning to gather force. Unfortunately, this "dumb bunny" was totally unprepared for the powerful spiritual upheaval that was about to take place. Because I had never taken the time to investigate the possible consequences of Kundalini meditation, I was not at all ready for the volcanic spiritual fallout that would soon visit me.

As had become my practice during meditation sessions, I once again visualized the coiling serpent moving gently through my body. In just moments, I began to feel a sense of peace. During past meditations, after attaining this place of calm, I would end my visualization and then lie back on a stack of fluffy pillows, enjoying the tranquility I had found. This time was different. Instead of submerging myself in the after-meditation serenity, I continued visualizing the "Rise of Kundalini Energy." "Something" was pushing me to stay with it, instead of ending my meditation session.

As I continued to visualize pulling vibrant streams of red energy up from my root chakra (tail bone) to my crown chakra (top of the head), my body began to tense. Suddenly, I could feel movement, intense movement, up my spine. This amazing feeling continued for several minutes. At the same time, a sensation of pressure at the top of my head began to build. Then, without warning, I felt an incredibly strong "crack" in the top of my skull. The sound of the crack vibrated through my ears, and for a moment I thought, "Oh my God! What have I done now?"

With this crack sound came a variety of new sensations. Sitting on my stack of pillows, with my spine as straight as an arrow, I felt just like an electrical conductor, plugged into an unlimited source of energy. Visions of swirling pastels—yellow, pink, blue, and orange—filled my head. Then I saw a multitude of stars and brilliant streams of light. The brightly colored visions were followed by an overwhelming buzzing sensation, and I felt electrified.

I was energized for the rest of the day, and for a number of nights afterward I only required three to four hours of sleep. It was an amazing feeling, but this wasn't the only outcome. Days later, I noticed other changes, strange changes that I was at a loss to explain. Doing therapy sessions with clients at the office became difficult, as I found myself distracted. The energy field, or aura, around people, plants, and even stones became visible to my naked eye. I found this absolutely fascinating. As the mood of an individual changed, so did the color of his or her energy field. Periodically, I would hear my clients say, "Carla? Carla? Hello? Is anyone in there? Are you listening to me? Earth to Carla! Where are you?" Where was I indeed!

Over the next two years, I wrote five books in a row, one right after the other, without taking a breather. My mind was a constant whirl of thoughts and new ideas. After putting Aaron, my only son at the time, to bed, I would stay up until 2, 3, or 4:00 A.M., writing. It was as if I had tapped into some creative source residing beyond me. After spending hours stringing words into sentences and sentences into paragraphs, I would stop, read what I had written, and with tears in my eyes ask, "Now just where did that come from?"

During such moments, I would feel overwhelmed with emotion, connected to every person, place, and thing in the universe. Blending into the sea of life felt glorious. It was as if my life essence was not encased within a physical body. With out-stretched fingertips, I would feel myself unite with every living thing around me. I could almost see the web of spiritual energy that connected the entire universe. At these emotionally life-altering times, the purpose of my existence would ring clearly, and like the ancient yogis, I would taste a second or two of pure bliss.

Where Do I Go from Here?

Though my creative energy seemed boundless, and the split-second interludes of spiritual enlightenment provided moments of "Ah ha!" there was a terrible downside to all of this. After the "crack," my entire concept of the world around me was rocked to the core. Every aspect of my being was dramatically impacted. I suddenly became very sensitive to bright light. Normal sunlight hurt my head, and the bright lights in department and grocery stores left me feeling irritable and agitated. I never left the house without at least two pairs of sunglasses. People would even see me wearing dark shades on overcast days or in the rain.

Loud noises, be it a radio, television, ringing phone, overbearing voice, banging washing machine, or bouncing dishwasher, gave me pounding headaches. In past years, headaches had never been a complaint of mine. Suddenly, I found myself carrying two well-known herbal headache remedies with me wherever I went. The herbs, feverfew and white willow, have been used for centuries to treat head pain, but if these didn't do the trick, I was off to the drugstore in search of more modern cures. Food became a real issue as I began to feel very uncomfortable eating meat. I vowed I would never become one of those miso-soup drinking, self-righteous vegetarians, but eating meat left me feeling sad and confused.

Out of the blue, the whole "God" thing became most perplexing. The God of my youth and early adulthood no longer made any sense to me. Years before, I had adopted a "New Age" form of God, and this concept now seemed self-serving in a very childlike way. With the "crack" came an increased influx of communication from deceased friends and relatives. These postcards from the afterlife descended upon me without warning. Because of this, I found myself tossing out my old ideas about God and the afterlife, yet I was at a loss when it came to knowing what would replace those old ideas.

My relationships with others also began to suffer. At times, I felt as if I were sitting on top of a mountain looking down on humanity. It was a lonely place to be. My poor husband was completely confused by my sudden transformation, and with great dismay, I felt disconnected not only from him, but from many of those around me. Because of this newfound sense of alienation, depression became a serious problem. "What has happened to me?" I wondered. "Now I don't fit in anywhere! No one understands me. I'm more out of control than ever, and I feel like a total freak!"

As time went on, the initial joy of what I thought had been spiritual growth gave way to a much darker side. Periodic bouts of intense emotion left me feeling as though I were losing my mind. Isolation set in, and I no longer wanted to remain on the planet. Physically, emotionally, and spiritually I had been ripped open, and for the life of me I did not know how I was going to glue myself back together again. At that point, I could have taken that step across the veil, from this life to the next, but self-destruction was not in my cards. There was work to be done and running to the afterlife wasn't going to solve anything.

Looking for Answers

Knowing my time on earth was not going to end anytime soon, I finally went looking, once again, for answers. Initially, during this next leg of my journey, I found even more confusion because, once again, I was looking in all the wrong places. Hindsight is always 20-20, and today I know my confusion was the beginning of my climb out of a deep, dark spiritual hole. But, at the time, this muddled emotional place seemed like one more laborious, steep mountain to climb with an unknown, dark valley lurking on the other side.

While sitting at lunch one day with a woman I had once considered to be a mentor, I shared my newfound ability to see auras. Her darkly lined eyes were piercing as she suggested with great nervousness that I get my own eyes checked for cataracts. Though my dear friend's concern was heartfelt, I knew she had not really "heard" me.

One friend, for whom I had great respect, told me I probably had a chemical imbalance and recommended I visit her shrink. This particular psychiatrist was well known to me and I knew if I told him I was seeing auras, making contact with deceased relatives, and having premonitions that more often than not came true, he would have loaded me up on a bunch of pretty pills. The medical profession was definitely not a safe group from which to seek guidance and support.

Most hurtful was the response of a woman friend with whom I had shared some of my deepest, darkest secrets. When I described the "crack" I had heard while doing Kundalini meditation, she became extremely frightened. Shortly after sharing with her, she announced to a group of my friends that I was practicing black magic, in trouble, and in need of serious salvation. An exorcism was even suggested! With such responses,

I decided enough was enough. No more looking to gurus or self-professed spiritual experts for answers. I needed a community of like-minded people in my life, peers with whom I could relate, and it was my responsibility to seek this out.

The Need to Know We Are Not Alone

By taking matters into my own hands, I soon discovered that I wasn't the "only one" having such experiences. After much searching, I found that many people like myself had been periodically "stepping into heaven" for centuries and that within our very own society, there were groups of people who celebrated such journeys.

For the next several years, I could be found in dark, metaphysical bookstores that reeked of incense, where the crystals outnumbered the people. On dusty bookshelves, I discovered a wealth of printed information that discussed profound spiritual experiences. Reading everything I could get my hands on, I soon discovered I was definitely not alone. While visiting these metaphysical haunts, I often met others who, like me, were just as bewildered and searching for answers. Slowly, the heavy veil of loneliness began to lift.

Over time, I built a support group of individuals with whom I could thrash out my spiritual adventures. Many of these men and women had also unknowingly walked down a variety of interesting spiritual paths, ill prepared for what was at the end of the road. Learning that there were others out there, just like me, struggling to understand their own clumsy leaps into an "unseen" world took away my deep sense of isolation and gave me hope.

Today, my support group is very large and it's made up of

people from all around the world. Each member of this group has had one or more profound spiritual experiences, and like me, they continue to walk, sometimes trudge, a road littered with a multitude of spiritual excursions. The comfort I take in being able to discuss such encounters openly has replaced my one-time sense of alienation with an eagerness to connect with those who are also looking for a place to "fit in." Nowadays, these brushes with the unknown even have a name, spiritually transformative experiences (STEs), and they are being investigated by competent researchers around the globe.

Perhaps you are one of those individuals who has caught a glimpse of the "unusual," and because of this, you are now feeling unique, unsupported, and alone. If so, I suspect you might not have shared your "otherworldly" encounters with many, fearing you'll face ridicule or that "Have you totally lost your mind?" look from friends and loved ones. You might be asking, "Who would understand? Who would believe me? What does this mean? Where do I go from here?"

Know that there are answers to all of these questions. There really are many positive, supportive solutions. Also, understand that you are not alone, just currently disconnected from those of us who appreciate how incredibly common STEs really are. Let me be one of the first to validate any spiritually transformative experiences you might have had.

If you haven't had an STE, maybe you are one of those seekers who is seeking knowledge of such experiences, but is fearful of openly discussing these topics. When asking questions about angels, visitations from deceased relatives, contact with celestial beings, premonitions about future events, lucid dreams, meditation experiences, seeing what others cannot see, and feeling what others cannot feel, we are often viewed as "weird," "eccentric," and "strange," or accused of dabbling in "black magic" or going against certain prescribed religious doctrines.

Possibly you have tried to investigate STEs on your own and have found the information in archaic books to be either very complicated or too narrow in focus. Know that such encounters come in many shapes and forms. Just because you haven't encountered an STE doesn't mean you aren't spiritual enough, you are traveling the wrong path, or you aren't trying hard enough to achieve such an experience. You don't need to hike up to a monastery high in the Himalayas and eat nothing but cold rice. You also don't have to follow a specific religious belief system, diet, exercise program, meditation practice, guru, meta-physical teacher, or leader to have spiritual adventures.

STEs can be found in all religious traditions and in every culture across the planet. Sadly, these life-changing events are rarely discussed in open society. It is this lack of discussion that is responsible for the isolation and confusion so many of us feel with regard to STEs.

Finding Our Place: The Key to Feeling We Fit

When an emotional, physical, or sexual abuse survivor visits my office for the first time, they are typically plagued by a number of symptoms of trauma. Often, other healthcare providers have misdiagnosed these symptoms. This can perpetuate a fear of sharing the trauma. The fear sets up a sense of shame, alien-ation, and uniqueness (no one understands me); and this can lead to confusion, depression, addiction, spiritual distancing, poor relationships, low self-esteem, rage at the world in general, sleep difficulties, and a host of other life problems. When an individual such as this hears me, a professional who has also battled addiction and waded through the pain of sexual trauma, tell them that these symptoms are normal, I can see the weight of confusion lift and a spark of hope flash in their eyes. The word "normal" is like a soothing balm for a despairing heart.

If a person walks into my office to share a deathbed vision, out-of-body experience, sense of "oneness" with the universe, near-death experience, Kundalini or meditative-induced intense encounter, vision of an angel, after-death communication, or any other intense spiritual experience, initially, they might be cautious, confused, and overwhelmed. They often feel misunderstood, depressed, raw with emotion, and isolated, and they sometimes struggle with sleep difficulties. Some of these people will also share that they have difficulty feeling connected to those they love. Along with this, feeling over-energized often creates concern. When I tell these seekers that such sensations are "normal" and will pass in time, relief spills over them. Providing loving support and helping these seekers to understand that these feelings are normal are essential for healthy integration and appreciation of any STE.

Sadly, today many who have had such experiences continue to feel very alone and fearful of sharing. All of us need support and understanding. This is the bond that not only connects us and grounds us, but also enables us to appreciate the mystery and wonder of our otherworldly jaunts. Unfortunately, most of us do not know that there are others "out there" who are just like us. Many so-called "New Age" groups preach a specific belief system, can be very exclusive and rigid, or insist on devotion to a particular guru or spiritual leader. Traditional religious institutions and the clergy tend to ignore such experiences altogether or accuse those who have had these experiences of "falling off the righteous path" and "playing into the hands of Satan."

Many mental health professionals, upon hearing phrases like "heavenly visions of another realm of existence," "vivid, colorful auras," or "communicating with celestial beings," immediately begin thinking that "delusional thought processes" and "mental illness" are involved. Most medical personnel don't take the time to pay close attention to what is being said. Instead, they are quick to whip out the prescription pad for an antidepressant or anti-anxiety medication, or worse, an anti-psychotic drug with terrible side effects!

When a powerful spiritual experience visits us, what do we do next? How can we discover whether or not others have had such encounters? To whom can we turn? For our own protection, must we tuck away our STEs and keep them from public view? And if we do this, how will we ever make sense of such experiences and integrate them into the fabric of our everyday lives?

I have always believed that life is not a "me" experience, but a "we" journey. The sensation of aloneness is but an illusion perpetuated by the belief that "no one understands me." This illusion is not only false, but also destructive to spiritual growth. I have had numerous STEs, and they have come in a wide variety of shapes and sizes. Every time I think no one can possibly understand what I have been through, a new teacher with an answer to my dilemma appears. Today, my teachers are not gurus, bestselling New Age authors, or self-appointed spiritual leaders. My teachers come in the guise of friends, coworkers, and even passing acquaintances. Whenever I encounter one of them, I am once again reminded that I am not alone.

Society does not yet feel at ease talking openly about such adventures. In recent years, our scientifically based, materialistic culture has not been very supportive of those who have such experiences. Most STE-ers who share openly find themselves relegated to the stature of tabloid comedy or are made light of and belittled. Others find themselves alone with their treasures, protective and secretive. In spite of such societal reactions, know as an experiencer or seeker that you are not alone. If you have been asking yourself, "Am I the only one?" come with me and meet my friends. These dear people have all asked the same questions you might be pondering. As we journey together, exploring the variety of STEs there are to encounter, you will quickly realize that such experiences are not so unusual. Everyday people from all walks of life are stepping into heaven and glimpsing the unseen, every single day.

chapter two

A Peek into the Future— "Where Did That Come From?"

"I always call Chris (my son) from the airplane
and tell him which flight I'm checked-in on.
He can tell me whether the flight's going to be
bumpy, whether it's going to arrive on time or
be delayed. He's had bad 'vibes' and that's
good enough for me. I'm grateful for Chris's
ability, whatever it is."[1]

—Robert Mitchum, actor (1917–1997)

Not as Uncommon as We Think!

*B*efore answering a ringing telephone, do you already know who is calling? Upon picking up the phone, have you then found yourself saying, "Oh my goodness! I was just thinking about you! Isn't that strange?" The caller might be a person you haven't heard from in years. What about the "sudden" urge to check on children in another room, only to find a young tot is about to stick a bobby pin into an electrical socket, get into some poisonous cleaning solution, or drink a bottle of perfume? If there is a knock at the front door, have you ever intuitively "known" before opening the door just who you would see standing on your front porch?

What about those so-called hunches and unseen "nudges"? How often have you heard or said to yourself, "I can feel it in my bones. Everything seems 'kosher,' but still something about this situation just doesn't feel right," only to discover that your hunch was on target? That's when you probably think back and say to yourself, "You know, I knew something terrible was about to happen, but I just couldn't put my finger on it."

I have an old dictionary that weighs at least fifty pounds. The thing is huge, it smells very musty, and it was written before I was even born. For years I have depended on this 1926 antique doorstop-in-print for the proper definitions of words. I hoisted up my old friend the dictionary and looked up the following terms: "premonition," "precognition," and "hunch." Interestingly, all of these words have several definitions in common, such as "foreknown," "foretold," and "intuitive impression that something will happen."[2]

Through the years, a multitude of titles have been given to individuals who have had the ability to foretell the future. Psychic, sage, prophet, diviner, shaman, soothsayer, oracle, intuitive, fortune-teller, witch, seer, mystic, and clairvoyant are just a few of the names history has given to those people who have glimpsed life trials yet to come. Is this ability a gift given to just a few, or are these common experiences many of us have had? In order to be true experiencers of premonitions and precognition, must we have the words "Intuitive Oracle" stamped in gold on our business cards?

Just how common are these hunches, intuitive feelings, and gut sensations? According to British author Michael Munn, a 1992 study in Canada discovered such experiences are more common than we think. Five hundred and two people were asked whether or not they had ever had a dream that predicted a future event. A full 17.8 percent—over 75 of these folks—said yes, they had experienced precognition dreams.[3]

I believe messages from the unseen world visit many of us. Premonitions are not familiar to only a select few. If this is the case, why are we as a culture so unaware of these experiences? Over the last few decades, only a very few in society have been willing to talk openly about their premonitions. As a result of this, the rest of us might not have known that our own experiences are not that unusual.

Premonitions Foretelling a Most Famous Disaster at Sea

Premonitions have been with us since the beginning of time. Over the centuries, many well-known historical events have been predicted with uncanny accuracy. One such tragedy even became the subject for a blockbuster Hollywood love story.

History buffs are very familiar with the disastrous demise of the luxury ship *Titanic*. Built to be "unsinkable," the *Titanic* was set to sail out of Southampton at high noon on April 10, 1912. Boarded by members of American and European high society with names like Rothschild, Astor, and Guggenheim, this floating tribute to opulence at its best was bound for New York City. With its Turkish bath, swimming pool, top-notch restaurants, squash court, and mechanical horse in the gymnasium, whose sole purpose was to keep the elite horsy riding set fit while at sea, this lavish liner was believed to be not only safe, but also the most modern ship of its time.

Sadly, seamen specially trained to keep lookout on the mast of the *Titanic* were ill prepared. Days before the impressive ship set sail, the binoculars needed to spot icebergs floating in the ocean had been misplaced. Out in the frigid North Atlantic Sea, using only the naked eye, lookout seaman Fredrick Fleet spotted the iceberg, which would be the *Titanic*'s doom, just thirty-seven seconds before its impact. On April 14, 1912, this catastrophe took the lives of more than 1,500 souls, setting the stage for decades of debate as to why this supposedly unsinkable, majestic beauty sank to the bottom of the ocean. Interestingly, this historical disaster not only represents one of the most devastating tragedies at sea, it also presents one of the strongest cases for premonitions of disaster.

According to one researcher, after the *Titanic* sank, it was discovered that there had been a huge number of premonitions about the ship's icy fate. Investigators of the time were shocked to learn that well over fifty accounts predicted the sea wreck before the ship even set sail. In Preston Dennet's article, "Do Tragic Events Cast Shadows Before Them?" we read the following.

Acting on a Hunch

"Several people went as far as to act on their premonitions and canceled their passage. Second engineer Colin MacDonald declined his position on the *Titanic* because of a 'hunch' that disaster lay ahead. Even some of the rich and famous passengers felt something was amiss. J. P. Morgan and Vanderbilt both cancelled their passage admitting to the superstitious fear of being on a ship's maiden voyage."[4]

Upon reading this, one might say, "Oh! That's just a coincidence!" or "I don't see any hard-core, specific information predicting just how the *Titanic* would sink. I'm going to need a little more than superstitious fear to convince me that someone actually had a premonition about this ship's inevitable plight." If this is how you are feeling, let me offer you one of the most detailed precognitive accounts of the *Titanic*'s eventual tragedy at sea on record.

A Premonition in Writing

At the turn of the twentieth century, there was a journalist and author named William Thomas Stead. During his day, Stead had his own publication called *Review of Reviews*. Before the sinking of the *Titanic*, Stead published an amazing story in this magazine.

     ॐ It was in this magazine that a story appeared written by Stead, called "From the Old World to the New." In it he set a scene on a liner crossing the Atlantic. The ship was the White Star liner Majestic, that at that time was commanded by Captain Smith, the very same officer who went down with his later ship the Titanic. In the tale Stead dwelt at great length on the dangers of icebergs in the Atlantic and had the Majestic driving through fog into the floe ice until, all of a sudden, the fog lifts and reveals a "dazzling array of icebergs, ever shifting and moving. Now and again a great berg would capsize with a reverberant roar." . . . One phrase in the story was ominous. "The ocean bed beneath the run of the liners is strewn with the whitening bones of thousands who have taken their passages as we have done, but who never saw their destination."[5]

This tale of a sinking ship might be seen as predicting future events to come, but in spite of this, the skeptical mind might say, "So, a story was written about a ship lost at sea. Smith, the name of the captain in the tale, is a common name. It's a bit of a stretch to think this has any connection to the Captain Smith who was on the *Titanic*." I might consider this conclusion, too, if it were the end of the tale, but it isn't. There is more to this story. Not only did Stead write a tale about a ship hitting an iceberg and sinking into the sea, he was the victim of such a disaster. At the invitation of President William Howard Taft, the journalist Stead set sail for America on the *Titanic*.

Stead's tale of a sinking ship isn't the only premonition in print that can be tied to his ill-fated trip on the *Titanic*.

     For an article on palmistry that appeared in Pearson's Magazine for January 1897 expert Mr. Robert Machray examined Stead's hand and reproduced a photograph of it. He stated that the "lifeline is moderately long, terminating about 63." That was precisely Stead's age at the time of the *Titanic* disaster. Stead had often expressed the opinion that he would die a violent death.[6]

Several individuals, independent of one another, also received "warnings" about the journalist's upcoming involvement with this most famous shipwreck. Before his trip, Stead was walking in the strand of London with another young writer named Shaw Desmond. As Mr. Stead shared his excitement about his upcoming adventure on the *Titanic*, Desmond was overtaken with a strong premonition of doom. The poor man was seized by an overwhelming "knowing" that the mentor with whom he was pleasantly strolling would soon be dead. Mr. Desmond never shared his fear with Mr. Stead. When word of the liner's tragedy reached him, he heard that Mr. Stead had survived. In spite of this, Mr. Desmond knew intuitively that his friend had passed on, and several days later, this fact was confirmed.

Finally, as if the above premonitions for disaster were not enough, Stead had also received three separate precognitive warnings about the *Titanic*'s demise before he ever set foot on the ship.

      ᐡ One was that "travel would be dangerous in the month of April, 1912." Another told Stead that he would be involved "in the midst of a catastrophe on water" involving the deaths of more than a thousand people. One clergyman, upon hearing about the building of the *Titanic*, was so moved by his own premonitions that he wrote to Stead predicting that the *Titanic* would sink. Despite all of these warnings, Stead booked passage on the *Titanic*, and died in the disaster.[7]

Mr. Stead did not heed the hunches, forewarnings, or intuitive concerns of others. Nor did he even consider that his own tale of a sinking luxury liner might be a warning to him regarding his own future travel by sea.

Unlike Stead's tale, not all premonitions have unhappy endings. Around the time of the *Titanic* tragedy, a young soldier received a premonitory nudge that saved his life. While at battle, a vision of his beloved mother kept him from certain death. This next account comes from a letter written by the soldier to his mother, published originally at the height of the Great War in 1918. From the book titled *Psychical Phenomena and the War*, by Hereward Carrington, Ph.D., we read the following.

      ᐡ One night while carrying bombs, I had occasion to take cover, when about twenty yards off I saw you looking toward me as plain as life. Leaving my bombs I crawled to the place where your vision appeared, when a German shell dropped on them (the other soldiers), and—well—I had to return for some more (bombs). But had it not been for you, I certainly would have been reported "missing." . . . You'll turn up again, won't you, mother, next time a shell is coming?[8]

This soldier trusted his gut and knew instinctively that the vision of his mother had saved him from certain death. How many of us ignore those small psychic messages, which say, "Look out!" or "Be aware!" Modern science has many of us convinced that belief in such extrasensory encounters is the byproduct of superstition and should be seen as ridiculous. Instead of integrating such experiences into our lifestyle, learning to trust these little invisible pushes and, at times, forceful "shoves," we sweep such warnings aside and try to carry on with only the guidance of our five basic senses. Learning to "listen" to premonitions can actually make life easier not only for us, but for those around us. The following account makes a case for "listening" to our premonitions.

Trusting Our Own God-Given Intuition

"February of 1997 I woke up in Atlanta, where I live and told my husband that we needed to go see my grandma in Detroit in October, because she was going to die then. My husband thought I was nuts. Several months later, during the summer, my dad called and said that Grandma most likely had only one more day to live and added that she most likely wouldn't make it through the night. He then said I needed to begin preparing immediately to come to Detroit for her funeral. I meditated on what he had said, and then called my dad back. I told him she would not die quite yet, but would instead get better and go back to the nursing home. I then told him she was going to die in October and that I would see him then. He too initially thought I was nuts. I also wrote this to him in a letter, which he kept.

"Well, everything I said happened. In October, I flew to Detroit to run a marathon and, after the race, told my husband, 'This is the time.' We went to visit my grandma. While visiting, she looked at me, shed a tear, and then passed on."

In the above account, the woman from Atlanta went against societal beliefs that say, "premonitions are just the consequence of an overactive imagination. Such flights of fantasy need to be overlooked, conquered, and ignored." Because she trusted her nudge from the beyond and ignored society's current stand on precognitive experiences, she was able to be with her beloved grandmother at the moment of her passing.

After reading this account, I thought to myself, "Instead of giving up her reality in order to accommodate the belief systems of those around her, this brave woman stuck to her guns and trusted her own internal 'God voice'." So many of us fear listening to that "sixth sense." For numerous years, I too ignored such messages because I was afraid of what other people would say.

When my second son, Josh, was born, I had a powerful premonition about my career as an author. A voice in my head kept telling me over and over again, "Your priorities must change for the time being. You will not publish another book until Joshua is five years old, so don't even try. Your energies are needed elsewhere." Did I listen? No! I hooked into the reality of a number of other people who said, "You must try to publish the manuscript you were working on before Joshua was born." For years I beat my head against a wall, rewriting several times a book that, in the end, was going nowhere. Whenever I became depressed about the lack of progress I was making, that voice was always there, telling me again that I would not publish another book until my son was in kindergarten. Eventually, after pushing against the will of what was to be, I found myself yelling back at the voice, "All right! I get it. I give up! I will quit!" The year Joshua went to kindergarten, I published two books. Imagine just how much stress I could have avoided if I had only listened to my own premonition.

As mentioned earlier, trusting our hunches can be life saving. On May 7, 1915, another luxury liner sank into the ocean. This British ship *Lusitania* was crossing the Atlantic when the Germans torpedoed it. Nearly 1,200 passengers lost their lives. In spite of the popular belief at the time that the Germans would never attack a ship full of passengers, one man went against this common thought and "listened" to his premonition.

     ∿ The strongest premonition came from successful shoe dealer Edward Bowen of Boston, Massachusetts. Bowen had booked passage on the *Lusitania*, but on the day before sailing, became unaccountably concerned. He canceled his passage. Later he told friends, "A feeling grew upon me that something was going to happen to the *Lusitania*. I talked it over with Mrs. Bowen and we decided to cancel our passage—although I had an important business engagement in London.[9]

How do we learn to trust our premonitions and act on them? Often times we must "unlearn" old belief systems. This can take time. Experience can be a great teacher for many of us.

After ignoring numerous warnings over the years in the form of visions, dreams, and little psychic tugs, Hollywood beauty Sophia Loren was finally able to "hear" and act upon one very crucial premonition.

Heeding a Warning

The Italian actress has had many premonitions, but initially she would not listen to them. Thankfully she listened to this one.

> ∾ She [Sofia] had "an overwhelming feeling of impending disaster" shortly before she was due to fly from Rome to Brussels to attend a gala charity ball . . . she heeded the premonition and cancelled. The organizers felt put out at having their big star let them down, but they found a replacement, Marcella Mariani, a former Miss Italy and aspiring actress.
>
> She traveled to Brussels on the plane Sophia would have caught and again back to Rome on the airplane that would have brought Loren back. Except on the return journey, the plane crashed. There were no survivors . . . She says that if she had heeded more of her premonitions, she could have avoided disasters like robberies and fires . . .[10]

Where do these precognitions come from, what is it that keeps us from listening to them, why are so few of us willing to take note of these clairvoyant messages, and how can we learn to be more receptive? I have a few answers to these questions and I'd like to share them with you.

When children are very small, they do not trust their own senses. This is part of being a child. While my father-in-law was passing, my two sons would come to me and ask, "Is Da [this is what they called their grandfather] going to die? He doesn't look very good, does he?" In this situation, my boys "knew" intuitively that their grandfather was preparing to leave this life. What they needed from me was validation of what they perceived, and I tenderly gave them this.

How often I have worked with parents who have invalidated their children's observations, fearing such young minds are incapable of dealing with reality. In spite of their own perceptions, children will typically trust what an adult says because caretakers are naturally in a position of authority. In a child's mind, the thought is, "Well, Mom is much bigger than I am. She takes care of me and knows more. Even though my grandpa looks like he is dying and I feel like he is dying, if Mom says he isn't, I will believe her."

Parents believe they are protecting children, doing what is in the children's best interest, when they invalidate what is being perceived. But this invalidation of the senses can spill over into adulthood. Instead of paying attention to our own inner voice, we often find ourselves listening to what is presented by those in positions of authority, within religious organizations, governmental situations, and even learning institutions. We, in essence, "forget" how to trust our own sixth sense.

It is very important for parents to learn to have more faith in their own premonitions and hunches. If you had a caretaker in childhood who was able to utilize those forewarnings received from dreams, visions, or emotional sensations, most likely, you will be more apt to acknowledge such unseen guidance.

The legendary actress Bette Davis grew up with a parent who was very accepting of a sixth sense. The following is an intriguing account from the blond-haired beauty with the exotic eyes. Most likely this was at the base of Ms. Davis's acceptance of the power of premonitions.

A MOTHER'S PREMONITION

Mother was very old-fashioned even for her day. But one evening, after much persuasion from me, I was allowed to accept a date with a boy alone. He brought two friends with him, and they brought a number of bottles of liquor, which they didn't tell my mother about. My young man and his friends were soon drunk and I was frantically trying to decide how to get away from them and not have to ride in the car with one of them drunk driving.

That evening, Mother went to see a play and happened to sit next to a beau of mine, Dick Thomas, and during the middle of the third act she had a premonition that I was in trouble and leaned over and asked him if he would drive immediately to the Bonnebunkport Hotel to collect me and bring me home.

Dick arrived and announced he was taking me home, which relieved me because I was in a dilemma as to how to get there. In the car, Dick told me that my Mother had sent him because she had had a premonition that something terrible was going to happen to me.

The next morning my escort from the night before came to see me. He was absolutely white and cold stone sober. He threw his arms around Mother and said, "Thank God you sent for Bette last night. One of my friends drove the car home and completely smashed it up. Bette most likely would have been killed." [11]

Even if our precognitions are not always right, it is important to give them at least a bit of attention. We can do this in two ways. First, we must understand the difference between a fear and a premonition. As we learn to pay more attention to our emotional-psychic-spiritual red-flag alerts, the better prepared we will be to decipher the difference between fears and true premonitions. A true forewarning tends to be powerful in emotion and directed at one particular circumstance or event in time. For instance, I don't have a fear of flying, but if while preparing for a trip by plane, I were suddenly hit with sudden uneasiness about the flight, I would pay attention. Today, I trust my sixth sense.

For many of us, having faith in these little nudges often requires proof that they do indeed pan out. My second suggestion is to write down on a calendar the date of every premonition, hunch, or precognitive dream you have for about six months. I do this on a regular basis. Then, see if in time it comes true. If your premonition is manifested in the future, be sure to write this date on your calendar also. When we can truly trust our invisible messages and are able to integrate these little gifts into our everyday living experience, we will find we move more in flow with the universe and cycle of life.

Visions and sensations of things to come can also enable us to be better prepared to serve those we love during their time of need. Marjorie's premonition did just that.

In the Right Place at the Right Time

ᐤ Marjorie was suffering from monthly female discomfort. A friend of hers offered her some medication to ease her pain. Upon taking the over-the-counter medication, she was struck with the thought that the pills would kill her. In spite of this "warning," she took them anyway.

After a while, Marjorie began to feel strange. She

thought, "What if my hunch were true? But it can't be true. You can't die from Midol [the medication]." Strangely, she felt peaceful—not afraid . . .

Suddenly Marjorie felt a tingling sensation. She floated upward and saw herself lying on the sofa completely immobile. At first she was scared, but soon that feeling disappeared. By this time, Marjorie was feeling wonderful. There was love, peace, and euphoria—incredible bliss—and she did not want to return . . . She (then) saw an unknown, dark-haired woman living in an unknown house. There was a three-year-old boy playing with a plastic toy he was about to swallow. The woman rushed in and saved him. Next, the same woman was watching another little boy on a monkey bar fall into a pool. She rushed and saved him. Finally, the same woman saw an infant who was about to put a screwdriver into his eye. The woman saved him.

. . . Amazingly the vision of the house and the woman with dark hair saving the three children came true. Marjorie (eventually) dyed her hair black and saved her three nephews (who hadn't yet been born when she had her vision) in the same house and in the same manner as had occurred in the vision.[12]

Unknown to Marjorie, her friend had not given her the common over-the-counter remedy for menstrual pain. Instead, she had been given a powerful narcotic, and Marjorie had had a serious allergic reaction to the medication. This reaction had brought her close to death, inducing what is called a near-death experience, or NDE (I will be discussing this phenomenon in more detail later). During this NDE, Marjorie had a premonition about events to come. In spite of the fact that she had received a warning before taking the medication, one telling her that it would kill her, Marjorie's NDE vision prepared her for life trials yet to come.

Premonitions of Spirits Waiting to Be Born

Premonitions can prepare us for other life events as well. My favorite type of precognitive dream involves that of spirits waiting to be birthed into the physical plane. In the above premonition, we saw how Marjorie had very specific visions of her nephews who had not yet been born.

Often, pregnant mothers will share, "I just know this child is going to be a girl," or "I had better starting thinking of 'boy' names. Something tells me this baby will be dressed in blue!" When the baby is born, many times the mother's intuition is right on target. Sadly, a mother's family, friends, or doctors frequently brush off such hunches, calling them lucky guesses. Pre-birth premonitions are very common and a few of the scientifically minded are finally standing up and taking notice of this phenomenon. Here is what researchers at John Hopkins University had to share with *Time* magazine in June 2000.

Dreaming of Baby

When it comes to predicting the gender of an unborn baby, mothers just might know best. Researchers at Johns Hopkins University interviewed 104 pregnant women who had chosen not to learn their babies' gender through prenatal testing. The mothers-to-be were asked to foretell whether they were carrying a girl or boy and to describe whether their guess was based on folklore, the way they were carrying the baby, a dream, or just a feeling. Of the women who based their forecast on a feeling or dream, 71 percent were correct, and all the women who cited a dream were right. Researchers concluded that there is much about the maternal-fetal connection to be explored.[13]

Like Marjorie's account, there are numerous documented premonitions regarding the future birth of children. The most interesting of these comes from mothers who have been told by doctors that they will never have children of their own. The following is a letter I received from a woman who had just such an experience.

BEFORE-BIRTH COMMUNICATION

Have you ever heard of "Before-Birth Communication"? I'm asking you because I had one before my daughter was born. It was a few years before her birth. It was so real. [In a dream] I remember that I was walking through a beautiful green field. At the top of a hill was a faded old farmhouse. As I got closer to the farmhouse, this little girl started to walk down the hill to meet me halfway. I was really concerned because here we were, in the middle of what seemed like nowhere, and this little girl was all alone. We met and she took my hand and looked up at me and I looked down at her. I asked her where her Mom was and whose little girl she was. She replied, I'm your little girl, Mommy, and I'm waiting for you." Well, as you can imagine, I was just blown away. I then thought, "This really is a dream as I can't have children." Needless to say, it's about ten years later and I not only have one beautiful daughter, but two lovely girls.

Many traditional scientists would have us all believe that our glimpses of events yet to come are just byproducts of chance, wishful thinking, or even delusional thought processes.

My question to such individuals is this: "How can you argue with the outcome of the above premonitions? Something is obviously going on and it can't be explained away by our five senses. Our known five senses can serve us well, but when we ignore the sixth sense, aren't we cheating ourselves?"

Learning how to trust our own "gut instincts," that God voice, the Higher Self, and those messages from the unseen world, allows us to begin using premonitions to our advantage, as tools. Such tools can improve the quality of our lives by connecting us with the spiritual essence living within each of us. As my very dear friend Morgan recently said, "Security must be found in the 'Invisible' or it will never be found at all." I tend to agree with him. How about you? Are you ready to pick up these tools?

chapter three

Death-Related Visions:
"Why Is She Here?
I Didn't Know She Had Died!"

"The boundaries between life and death are at best shadowy and vague. Who shall say where one ends and where the other begins?"

—Edgar Allen Poe, American writer (1809–1849)

*E*dgar Allen Poe couldn't have said it better. The boundary between our earthbound, bodily existence and life after the death of the physical self is very shadowy indeed. For hospice advocate Stephen Levine, the author of *Healing into Life and Death*, "Death is just a change in lifestyles."[1] I tend to agree with him. Nowhere is the doorway between life as we know it and continued existence, after the physical body returns to dust, more apparent than with death-related visions. This particular type of STE is probably the most common of all mystical encounters. The man who coined the term "death-related visions," medical doctor and famed near-death (NDE) researcher, Melvin Morse, had this to say about such occurrences.

ə I have found that death-related visions . . . are the most common paranormal events in our lives. So common are these visions that more than 10 percent of the population has had such a vision.[2]

Several decades ago, I began investigating a very specific type of death-related vision, called the deathbed vision, or DBV. Not only had I had such an encounter, but so had both my husband and my youngest son. In search of validation of what we as a family had encountered, I collected hundreds of similar stories. After pouring over one DBV account after another, I soon found these glimpses into an afterlife existence to be the most fascinating of all reported death-related visions. Eventually, I devoted an entire book to this phenomenon titled, *One Last Hug Before I Go: The Mystery and Meaning Behind Deathbed Visions*.

What exactly is a DBV? A deathbed vision is an "otherworldly" experience the dying and their family members often encounter just before a physical death occurs. Some dying individuals or those they love will report visions of angels, deceased loved ones, or religious figures moments, hours, days, or even weeks before actual death occurs. These visitations appear to be for the purpose of providing comfort to the dying. Along with this, DBV encounters ease grief for surviving loved ones.

Unknown to many in today's society, the DBV phenomenon has been with us throughout history. For instance, historical Jewish literature is chock full of narratives recounting the deathbed visions of famous rabbis. Those who buried Baal Shem Tov, the founder of the Hasidic movement (mid-eighteenth century), said they saw his soul leave the earth plane. "And those who buried Baal Shem Tov said they had seen his soul ascend toward the heavens as a blue flame."[3]

Christian literature is also rich in DBV information. From my book *One Last Hug Before I Go*, we read the following.

> ∾ In Christian literature, particularly in the oral traditions gathered and recorded between 55 C.E. and 100 C.E. a specific spiritual event is discussed repeatedly. The core of this even rests on the premonition of an upcoming death and is considered one of the most famous accounts given in the New Testament: Jesus of Nazareth predicting his own impending death to his followers. He tells them he knows his time of death is near and even foretells how his apostles will respond when the Romans arrest him.[4]

In 1923, a researcher and physician named Sir William Barrett brought together numerous accounts of deathbed visions and put them in a small book titled *Death Bed Visions*. Barrett's wife, also a physician, had a patient who reported an incredible vision. This account spurred the Barretts' interest in DBVs, and the two spent the rest of their lives researching not only the visions of the dying, but other related phenomena.

Almost forty years later, another researcher, Dr. Karlis Osis, decided to follow up on Barrett's DBV work with a pilot study of his own. He, too, made a number of interesting observations. Condensed from Osis's book, *At the Hour of Death*,[5] here are just a few of the findings this researcher made.

- Dr. Osis noted that people who were close to death or dying and had a DBV typically saw people who had already passed.
- He also discovered that these visitors came to the dying person to offer assistance in the dying process. Deceased

friends or relatives came to escort the dying person to an afterlife.

- One very interesting finding noted by Osis contradicts certain religious tenants. According to his research, previous religious beliefs did not appear to determine Who would have a DBV before dying. In other words, both believers and nonbelievers had powerful DBVs.

- In Osis's initial pilot study, patients who had DBVs were not on medications.

- With some cases, family members and friends at the deathbed also saw deceased relatives, friends, religious figures, or angels.

- Though Osis originally set out to prove that DBVs were only a byproduct of the dying process (hallucinations of a dying brain), he came away from his research with more questions than could be answered.

- Dr. Osis, like Dr. Barrett, decided these particular phenomena could not be so easily explained.

Sadly, in spite of the findings of Barrett, Osis, and Morse, as well as individuals such as myself, narrow-minded skeptical scientists, medical personnel, and mental-health practitioners have continued to dismiss the DBV experience. Much research and study is needed in order to understand the DBV experience more fully, but, sadly, grant money for such investigations is nonexistent.

As a result of this, many helping professionals quickly dismiss these comforting visions, which can ease the dying process, soothe grief, and encourage future personal spiritual development. Because I often am in the company of such closed-minded professionals, I had to find a way to throw a wrench into the middle of such narrow thinking. Interestingly, I found the solution sitting within my own collection of DBV accounts. By presenting a certain "type" of DBV, those that were often difficult, if not impossible to dismiss, I discovered the cynical person more often than not stopped debating and sat there looking rather confused!

Not long ago, I found myself on the Howard Stern radio show. Not only is this "shock jock" a well-known, closed-minded skeptic, he can also be most persistent in his attempts to prove that experiences of an "unseen nature" are the byproduct of, in his opinion, a delusional person. The following DBV account from Robin Abrams often throws the steel-trapped mind for a "momentary loop"! After sharing this particular DBV encounter with Stern, the popular cynic was actually speechless for a moment or two. See if Robin Abrams's dramatic account captivates you.

DAD KNEW MY BROTHER HAD PASSED ON AND WE NEVER TOLD HIM!

I witnessed firsthand my father's [Albert Abrams] "peek" into the afterlife. Due to a devastating stroke, he was confined to a bed in a nursing home . . . . One year after his stroke, to the date, my brother passed away. His death was most unexpected and premature. He was murdered. Before his untimely death, this brother generally visited my father anywhere from three to four times a month. We decided, as a family, to withhold the news of my brother's murder from my father for as long as possible. There is absolutely no way he could have known my brother had died.

In less than a week after my brother's death, my father said (very fluently, which was surprising because the stroke had affected his speech), "I used to have three children, now I only have two." We asked him, "Why did you say that, Dad?" And he looked at us as if we were nuts. If looks could speak, it was as if he were saying, "Don't play dumb!"

Prior to his death, my brother never visited my father more than once a week at the most, so not enough time between visits had occurred for my father to recognize that something was not right. I changed the subject immediately and that was the end of that exchange that day.

Two months or so before my father died, he finally told me that yes, my brother who had been murdered had come to visit him in (in a DBV) before he had received word that he had died. Along with this, my father made several references to receiving messages from my mother. She had been deceased for fifteen years. It is important for you to know that my father's mind, when awake, had never been sharper. I truly believe, with absolutely no doubt, that for a time, he had a foot in both worlds.

Just how did Mr. Abrams know his son was no longer living on the physical plane? No one had told him a thing about the brutal murder this young man had experienced. How did this event impact his daughter Robin? Here is what she had to say.

I am skeptical of many so-called "spiritual" or "New Age" concepts. However, from a personal experience I have no doubts or questions about an afterlife or the preparation for the afterlife prior or at the onset of death.

Today, Robin continues to delve into the mystery of her own spiritual essence and explore a particular religious path. Finally, her brother's killer was recently found guilty of second-degree murder, and he was sentenced to life in prison for his crime. As difficult as this horrific murder and the subsequent passing of her beloved father were on Robin, a DBV provided her with enough evidence to believe that physical death is not the end.

Is this type of death-related vision an isolated case? Are the dying visited by persons unknown to them to have passed? According to Barrett's research, the answer is "yes!" to both questions. Here is an account taken directly from Sir Barrett's 1926 collection of DBVs.

"OH, JEANNIE, I'M SO GLAD YOU ARE HERE!"

In a neighboring city were two little girls, Jeannie and Edith, one about eight years of age and the other but a little older. They were schoolmates and intimate friends. In June of 1889, both were taken ill with diphtheria. At noon on Wednesday Jeannie died. Then the parents of Edith, and her physician as well, took great pains to keep from her the fact that her little playmate was gone. They feared the effect of the knowledge on her own condition. To prove that they succeeded and that she did not know, it might be mentioned that on Saturday, June 8, at noon, just before she became unconscious of all that was passing about her, she selected two of her photographs to be sent to Jeannie, and also told her attendants to bid her goodbye.

She died at half-past six o'clock on the evening of Saturday, June the 8. She had roused and bidden her friends goodbye, and was talking of dying, and seemed to have no fear. She appeared to see one and another of friends she knew were dead. So far it was like other similar cases. But now suddenly, and with every appearance of surprise, she turned to her father and exclaimed, "Why, papa, I am going to take Jeannie with me!" Then she added, "Why, papa! You did not tell me that Jeannie was here!" And immediately she reached out her arms as if in welcome, and said, "Oh, Jeannie, I'm so glad you are here!"[6]

The loss of a child is a devastating experience for which no parent is ever prepared. In my work as a psychotherapist, I have counseled many bereaved parents. Protecting our little ones from the pain of life's tragedies is a parental instinct. In this particular situation, not only did Edith's mother and father work diligently at keeping the death of her playmate from her, her personal physician was also cautious. In spite of the lengths these loving caretakers went to shield this young child, Jeannie, the playmate, was there to escort her dear friend to an afterlife existence.

In my experience working with the bereaved, I can share that though the DBV doesn't eradicate grief, it does soothe loss and provide reassurance that the spirits of departed loved ones do go on. Most important, DBV visitations ease passage from this life to the next. Here is another account that makes this point perfectly clear. Natalie Kalmus, best known for her contribution to the development of Technicolor, was very ill. Her family decided not to tell her that her cousin Ruth had passed. Natalie's DBV visitation provided her sister Elenor with a shock.

"I AM GOING UP WITH THEM"

I sat on her bed and took her hand. It was on fire. Then Elenor seemed to rise up in bed, almost to a sitting position.

"Natalie," she said, "there are so many of them. There's Fred and Ruth—what's she doing here?"

An electric shock went through me. She had said Ruth! Ruth was her cousin, who had died suddenly a week before.

But I knew that Elenor had not been told of the sudden death. . . . I felt on the verge of some wonderful, almost frightening knowledge. . . .

Her voice was surprisingly clear. "It's so confusing. There are so many of them!" Suddenly her arms stretched out happily. "I am going up with them," she murmured.[7]

Notice how similar this 1955 DBV account is with the previous 1889 Barrett death-related vision. Now, compare both of these DBVs with Robin Abram's modern-day visitation. Can you detect the common similarities all three of these accounts have with one another? In each instance, the ill person is initially unaware that a beloved family member or friend has passed. Those at the bedside take great steps to protect this bedridden person from news about these losses. The consistent fear is that such news will depress the ill person and possibly quicken death. Finally, notice the surprised reaction those readying themselves for death express upon being visited by the person who has, unknowingly to them, recently passed.

In investigating DBVs of this nature, it is very apparent that the bonds that connect a loving family continue even after a death. A passing does not break the ties of love. This appears to be very true in cases involving siblings. Here is a modern-day DBV account that underscores the importance bonds of family love play even after physical death.

HE'S RIGHT HERE!

I lost my mom (several years ago). She was hospitalized for several months before she left this world. While my Mom was in the hospital dying, her eldest brother passed away. We elected not to tell my mother, as it would only upset her and perhaps speed up her death. However, the day after we learned of my Uncle's death, we were standing in my Mother's hospital room. Without opening her eyes—she'd had several strokes and opening her eyes just seemed too much effort for her—she said [calling her brother by a nickname] was here." [The nickname]—was the nickname of her eldest brother [the brother who had just passed]. She did not tell us the purpose of his visit, only that he came to see her.

In the above account, once again we see that the family decided not to share her brother's recent passing with this dying woman. Regardless of the efforts made to conceal this news, this mother "knew" her brother had left this world because he came to visit her. Let's look at a similar report written over 130 years ago. The father reporting this account to Sir Barrett was a respected man of the church who asked that his true identity not be disclosed.

"THERE IS LITTLE HARRY CALLING TO ME."

On November 2nd and 3rd, 1870, I lost my two eldest boys, David Edward and Harry, from scarlet fever, they being then three- and four-year-olds, respectively.

Harry died at Abbot's Langley on November 2, fourteen miles from my vicarage (this father was the Vicar of a church) at Aspley, David the following day at Aspley. About an hour before the death of this latter child (David) he sat up in bed, and pointing to the bottom of the bed said distinctly, "There is little Harry calling to me." Of the truth of this fact I am sure, and it was heard also by the nurse.

Signed X.Z. Vicar of H—[8]

The Vicar also added that he had taken great care in keeping the death of little Harry from his brother David. How can the dying know such things? I believe that we are the most psychically "in tune" with other realities of existence when we are on the brink of death. In ancient cultures, initiation into the schools of mystery often involved inducing death to bring on an otherworldly vision or contact with deceased loved ones living in an afterlife realm. Researcher Dr. Janet Cunningham gives us a peek into this ancient, often fatal, practice.

Bringing Death on for a Moment of Enlightenment

ॐ According to an Egyptian papyrus from approximately 225 A.D. . . . There is some evidence . . . that drugs or psychedelics were used to assist the initiate in undergoing the death and rebirth rituals, which were often fatal.

Esoteric writers . . . refer to neophytes and initiates in the Egyptian Mystery Schools who were taught about other dimensions of reality; the mystery teachings were done under a strict code of silence. All of these writers refer to secret initiations in which the initiate—if he or she lived— experienced other levels of reality while being out of the physical body. . . . the initiatory rites of the Osirian and other ancient Wisdom Schools have parallels with the near-death experiences that are occurring today. As people today describe the aftereffects of their near-death experiences, so it was with those few who survived Initiation: They knew, not from faith but through experience, that they were immortal.[9]

In other words, in centuries gone by, mystical schools had very extensive initiation rites. Bringing the new Initiate close to death with toxic herbs, drowning, or suffocation was a common rite-of-passage practice. Once the Initiate had in essence died, which in this case would involve a near-death experience, had received a vision, and had been reborn, he was then seen worthy of receiving the secret teachings of his particular Order or school of mysticism.

Using old-world methods, many of today's modern mystics attempt to sneak quick entry into the unseen world. While a friend of mine was digging sewer lines in Utah with his college buddies, he and his friends were asked to participate in a Native American Sing. He found himself on an Indian reservation, taking part in a sacred rite, which was honoring the recent death of a tribal member. Part of the ritual involved the ingestion of the hallucinogenic cactus, peyote. According to anthropologists, this funny-looking cactus has been used for inducing visions for 10,000 years. Consumption of this herb by Native Americans can be dated as far back as the 1600s.

My friend ate a piece of the brown stuff, and he found the taste to be rather sharp and very bitter. Its hallucinogenic effects impacted him little, so he decided just to sit back and watch the other participants. As singing and drumming went on throughout the night, those who continued to eat the herb experienced numerous visions. Visions play an integral part in Native American spirituality and they are taken very seriously. To this date, buttons of peyote continue to be consumed by numerous Native Americans in a time-honored, respectful ceremonial manner.

With regard to ancient traditional spiritual rituals, unlike my dear friend in Utah, one other acquaintance of mine had a very different experience. This either brave or foolish soul accepted an invitation to participate in a true vision quest ritual in a village deep in the jungles of Peru. During this ceremony, he was told he would meet up with either his spiritual guide or animal self. The ingestion of a vile concoction of herbs was to be the key that would open the door to his enlightenment. After drinking the nasty-tasting brew, he became violently ill and then vomited profusely. At that moment, he had felt very close to death. After his stomach calmed down, he did experience some very curious visions.

Modern-day death-related visions, along with DBVs from recent history, are validating what the initiates of the old schools of mystery went to great lengths to discover. Interestingly, unlike the induced near-fatal and often deadly initiation rights of antiquity, naturally being close to death can present just as many spiritual surprises. The following account is fascinating and it was reported just a few decades ago. Once again, we see that the bonds of love between two siblings can never be broken, even with physical death.

"HE WAS SO HAPPY AND SINGING"

On May 31, 1916, The *Queen Mary* was hit by German gunnery and it sank. About a week after the battle, the sister of one of the seamen who went down with the ship picked up a paper and saw that her brother was listed as one of the dead. Previously, she had been very ill and family had taken great caution in protecting her from the news of her brother's passing. A vision of her brother, on the exact day the ship sank, had forewarned her that something wasn't right.

I was very ill at the time. . . . I was taken worse and thought I was going to die. (In the vision) . . . I was with my brother on his ship and thought he was so happy and singing, and then it changed and he was at home on leave. I thought I repeatedly spoke to him each time but he did not speak to me. I knew I was ill, and thought he would not speak to me because I was disfigured. (The sister was suffering from erysipelas, a very severe inflammatory skin disorder and had been ill for some time.) I asked my mother if he had gone back and she said he had not been home. I said I knew he had, it seemed so real. I was very much upset because he would not speak to me. I did not hear of the sinking of the *Queen Mary* until a week after, as I was too ill for my mother to tell me . . . . It would be just about the time when the ship went down that I saw my brother, as it was late in the afternoon on Wednesday, May 31. (The battle began around 3 P.M. on May 31.)[10]

This sick girl not only had a vision of her brother on the ship moments before it was bombed, but then saw him at her home. This is a classic deathbed vision. With this type of vision, the person who is in the process of passing or has just died is frequently separated from family and friends by miles of distance. In spite of this distance, the surviving friend or family member experiences an awareness, dream, or vision telling them that "something" just isn't right with their loved one. A phone call, telegram, or letter announcing a death soon following these deathbed experiences then validates that a passing has occurred. With death-related visions of this nature, there is a sense that the invisible hands of the spirit taking flight reach out with love to those who will be left behind to say not only, "I love you," but "goodbye."

In this turn-of-the-twentieth-century account, we saw once again how someone close to death's doorway can receive a spiritual message about the passing of a loved one before there is actual knowledge of this loss. In the next modern-day account, we read how a dying person lived to tell a bedside caretaker about a special visitation from a recently departed loved one.

"NO, GO BACK!"

This particular man had gone into cardiac arrest and about fourteen minutes had elapsed before he was revived. He had experienced numerous cardiac arrests and finally had a permanent defibrillator implanted in his chest. [Upon revival] I immediately asked if he had had a vision of any type when he had died. He said he had. His niece, I believe, had appeared and said something to the effect of, "No, go back. One of us is enough." Upon hearing this, I assumed she had recently died. Eventually, I learned that she had died recently, but he was unaware of this. She was young and had been killed in a car accident. He found out about her death a week later.

Many researchers of modern-day death-related incidences refer to the above encounters as near-death experiences. In such instances, a person is either close to death or actually dies and is then brought back to life. Later on, I will share with you more specifically about the nature of this phenomenon. For the time being, it is important to note that here, once again, we have a modern-day example of a dying man having a vision of a loved one who, unbeknown to him, has just died. Modern medicine can now bring dying individuals back from the brink of death and, like the near-death-induced rituals of ancient mystics, modern survivors are also reporting visions of deceased loved ones. In reviewing the accounts presented in this chapter, we have to ask ourselves, "How can these dying people know about the recent deaths of others, which have not been shared with them?" As we begin to cross the threshold of physical death and move toward a spiritual existence, do we really have one foot in both worlds? And if so, why isn't modern science taking the time to investigate such encounters?

In my own lifetime I have had several deathbed visions. In each case, the person who was passing was miles away from me. When I was just sixteen, my own mother died at the young age of thirty-eight. As she lay dying in the hospital on an early spring morning, I was at home, buried under a stack of warm blankets, snoring away. At the exact moment of her departure from this world to the next, I awoke from my deep sleep and knew she had finally left this life. At this same time, two dear family friends, living in different locations, also found themselves rubbing the sleep out of their eyes and "sensing" deep within their very being that my mother, Carol, was no longer with us. As she shed her cancer-ridden body and made her way toward her next spiritual adventure, my mother gave all three of us an invisible, loving hug.

For years I was unable to appreciate this final gift from my mother. As a young teen, I could find no one with whom to talk about it. The adults around me invalidated this wonderful experience, so I tucked it deep inside. When I began my schooling in psychology, teachers reinforced that my encounter was just the byproduct of grief-induced, wishful thinking. Traditional science told me to put such encounters into the categories of tabloid news or mental illness. And, to top off these words of "educational wisdom," there were studies and theories inferring that no well-read, proper mental-healthcare provider would ever consider such "superstitious nonsense." In other words, it was no longer "safe" to "believe" in what I had experienced.

If you have had a death-related encounter, know that it was real. Find people to talk to who will be genuinely interested and who will support you. Realize that such experiences tend to create a great deal of emotion. They also force us to re-examine our belief in life after death, concepts of God or a Higher Power, and the purpose of our own living experience. We all have a purpose, but many of us have lost touch with this. The dramas, addictions, and distractions of life keep us from getting our priorities straight. We put those we love most on the back burner and give up our dreams. Spiritual development is sacrificed for a job we detest, and the special joys of loving relationships seem out of our grasp. Interestingly, the death of a loved one can force us back onto our own true path. Encountering a death-related vision such as those discussed above can be a potent wake-up call. When a door has been opened, it is important to take the risk and walk into the next room. Who knows what wonders await us?

chapter four

Out of the Mouths of Babes—
The STEs of Children

"Children are true believers, and some of us
are lucky enough to make the transition to
adulthood without losing the ability to see
through young eyes."

—Anne Geddes, internationally renowned
Australian-born photographer, 1996

*H*ow many of us can truly say the "awe" of our youth has
not been tarnished by the cynicism of adulthood? When
confronted with events that cannot be scientifically explained,
most of us tend to wrap ourselves quickly within a blanket of
skepticism. Recently, I was at a dinner party. It was a beautiful
affair situated in a historical building overlooking the turquoise
Gulf Coast water. As the evening wore on, I was asked about
my work. In response, I began to chat away about near-death
experiences, after-death communications, deathbed visions,
meditation, and premonitions.

With delight and excitement, I shared the results of a 1992
Gallop poll, which described how approximately 13 million
people in the United States have come close to death and
have had the sensation of leaving their bodies. For a near-death

experiencer, near death is brought on by illness, serious accident, medical procedures, surgery, allergic reactions, or other trauma. Appearing to be clinically dead to the medical staff attending them, once conscious, NDE-ers will often describe their soul separating from their physical body, traveling through a tunnel, visiting a heavenly place, reviewing their entire life, and being greeted by deceased relatives or beings of incredible, brilliant light. Profound, positive psychological and spiritual life changes can occur after an NDE encounter.

As I continued discussing the NDE with my assorted dinner companions, the eyes began to roll and the snickering became less than discrete. I then decided to blow them away with some after-death-communication findings. Dr. Raymond Moody, often considered the godfather of NDE research, stated in his book *Reunions* that 75 percent of parents who lose a child report some sort of after-death communication or vision of the child within a year after the youngster's death. A good friend of mine, Dianne Arcangel, validated Moody's results with her own investigations into after-death contact. In her 1997 article for *The American Journal of Psychical Research*, Dianne stated that 84 percent of those involved in her investigation had encountered visitations from departed loved ones.

My dinner buddies were still not impressed. Instead, I heard, "Carla, you really have lost your mind! How can you believe in all of this nonsense?"

"Enough," I thought to myself. It was time to pull out the big guns. In order to do this, I turned to the research of my friends Brad Steiger and Sherry Hansen Steiger.

Some More Interesting Numbers

Beginning in 1967, the Steigers sent out a questionnaire related to mystical experiences. In their 1999 book *Touched by Heaven's Light*, they reported that their questionnaire was distributed to almost 30,000 people. The results showed that:

> ∾ During an NDE . . . 76 percent reported that their soul left their body; . . . 57 percent claimed to have gone to a heavenly dimension or realm; and . . . 60 percent stated that they received an inspirational communication from a Higher Intelligence . . . as the result of an NDE or (out-of-body experience) OBE . . . 50 percent reported they had been aware of a guardian angel or guide; . . . 35 percent described having been blessed by the appearance of a holy figure; . . . 44 percent claimed to have communicated with the spirit of a departed loved one.[1]

After rattling off the above numbers, I smugly flashed my pearly white teeth and cracked a big Cheshire cat grin. "There!" I announced. "What do you think about those numbers?" I truly believed I had driven my point home.

"Woo woo science!" my doctor friend replied. Sitting directly across from me was a dear friend who was a hardcore, medically minded skeptic. "Those numbers mean nothing," he added as he lifted his wine glass to his lips. Shaking his head, he poked further fun at me by saying, "Carla, are you going to end tonight's festivities with a voodoo dance?"

This brought the entire table to hysterics, but I was still not giving up. "Okay," I said. "You really are a stubborn group. Close-minded to the core. Well, I'd like to share with you an after-death vision, which just might change your mind."

My doctor friend chuckled as he dove into a huge, rich piece of chocolate cake. "Nothing you can say will ever change my mind. Visions of deceased relatives, the soul separating from the body, predicting future events, all of this is just a bunch of hogwash." As he stuffed a hunk of creamy icing into his mouth, I said, "What about the otherworldly visions of children? Young children, untouched by societies' prejudices, skepticism, or tabloid news?" I then shared the following account, and afterwards, not a word was said.

THERE'S MY FRIEND!

I truly believe in life after death. . . . My [old] love passed over this summer. Timing was bad and I ended up marrying someone else [instead of the old love], but our love for each other never stopped . . . my two-year-old told my husband the day I left to go to his gravesite that "mommy is with a ghost," and when we were at the playground she said, "There's my friend [the name of the man who had passed]." My husband's mouth dropped, and I almost passed out because she said his last name, a name I don't think she ever heard!"

This is by far one of my favorite areas of spiritual investigation. Mystical experiences reported by children are typically spontaneous, innocent, free, and open. Childhood encounters are for the most part untouched by the biases and prejudices of society. Young children have not read books on topics related to premonitions, NDEs, or ADCs, nor have they spent hours in front of the television watching shows like "Crossing Over" with American medium John Edward, and for them, "meditation" is just another funny word. Because the mind of a child has yet to be tarnished by the media, religion, politics, or philosophical ideology, investigators like me find it difficult to ignore such pure, honest, and spur-of-the-moment spiritual accounts.

Sadly, those willing to listen to children talk about their wonderful encounters are rare. In our culture, if a child shares such experiences, usually they are quickly dismissed by surrounding adults, put on medication by mental-healthcare personnel, or seen as using fantasy in order to get attention. When adults do not validate a child's STE account, such incidences begin to fade away from memory and children learn not to trust their experiences.

In my private practice, I often hear about otherworldly encounters from young children. Years ago, a seven-year-old girl told me about a beautiful dream she had had. She tried sharing this dream with her mother, but was quickly told there was nothing to it. Because the dream had been so vivid, so incredibly unusual, it stuck with her. While she was on the floor of my office drawing with crayons, I noticed her colorful picture was full of big, luscious flowers. When I asked her about these wonderful flowers, much to my surprise, she shared the following.

HEAVEN IS A FIELD FULL OF FLOWERS

My grandmother had died and I was worried about her being in that box in the ground. I was afraid she was cold. Well, then I had this dream and my grandma was in it. She was in this field full of flowers, really big flowers, and the colors were super bright. Real bright, like not real. And she was smiling. She was so happy and she said I wasn't supposed to worry about her.

Though she had seen her grandmother's coffin lowered into the ground, her dream was telling her something else. The mother of this child was the daughter of the grandmother who had passed. As mentioned earlier, the mother was unable to comfortably talk with her own child about the dream. Eventually, I learned that her difficulty in "hearing" her daughter was related to her own unresolved grief and serious fear of death. My job as a therapist was to sort out the mother's pre-existing death phobia from the daughter's wonderful after-death communication or ADC.

What is interesting to note is that this young girl's dream has characteristics typical of an ADC experience. When an ADC comes in the form of a dream, colors are vividly intense and typically a deceased loved one comes with a message of comfort for the receiver. Such messages convey, "I'm fine! Don't worry about me!" or "I love you and am still here!"

The young girl who had the vision of her grandmother in a field full of flowers in heaven was very aware that this night-time visitation was not a normal dream and that there was something very unusual about it. It was important for me to validate for her that, yes, her dream was not only extraordinary, but similar to a vision reported by a ten-year-old girl dying of fever in 1864.

> ∞ . . . the heavenly flowers and trees that I love so much (are) here—for I see them, and they are more beautiful than anything you can imagine—they will be there.[2]

Children are typically very open with their otherworldly experiences. For them, such events are seen in an everyday light and are viewed as naturally as eating breakfast, getting dressed for the day, or rolling in the grass with a favorite pup. Children only become suspicious of such encounters when adults invalidate them.

In many instances, parents and caretakers become willing to believe their children when they themselves have been exposed to other realities. Once this happens, they can then hear about their children's experiences. This was the case for my extremely scientifically minded husband.

A VISITATION FROM AN ANGEL

1996 was a very, very hard year for my family. During this time, my husband, children, and I helped my father-in-law pass. "Da," as my two boys called him, was a six-foot-tall Frenchman who rescued a number of family members from concentration camps after the Holocaust. When he and my mother-in-law came to the States, Da began a successful career as an eye surgeon, while Mom worked as a professor at the local university.

My two sons loved their grandfather. Even after his stroke, which left him bedridden, the boys had no difficulty camping out on his bed, eating popcorn, and watching cartoons. Often, I would have to drag my boys away from Da's bedside. Grandfather and grandsons just had too much fun together.

Several weeks before my father-in-law's passing, my youngest son made an announcement. While traveling to the grocery store, he informed me that there was a "red-haired kid" sitting with him in the backseat of the car. I did a double take in the rearview mirror just to make sure Josh was alone with only his toy dinosaurs. Noting the empty seat beside my son, I decided to play along with what I thought, at the time, was one more three-year-old game.

"Honey, what's your friend's name?" I asked. While pulling at the legs of his dinosaur, Josh looked at the seat beside him and answered, "Who, him? That kid? His name is Damus."

A few days later, while running one more errand, Damus visited us again. Living on an island, we were making our way to a shop situated just across the street from the beach. As I coasted through a stoplight, I asked if Damus was still around. My son looked at me with much irritation, pointed at the seat beside him, and said, "Can't you see him? He is right here!" Once again, I looked in my rearview mirror to make sure I had not unwittingly picked up an unknown passenger. Though I could see nothing, except for my son's stack of plastic, vicious-looking toy creatures, eventually I learned that a third "being" truly was accompanying us from shop to shop.

"Sweetie, how long has Damus been around?" I asked, keeping one eye on the rearview mirror and another on the beachfront street.

"Oh, Damus just got here a few days ago," answered my son as he attacked the backseat with his fanged creature.

"Damus just got here?" I asked. "Is he a friend of yours?"

Still growling away, Josh said, "No, Mom! He just got here! He came here for Da!" . . .

It was Friday the thirteenth. We decided to take a break from the hospital and round up the boys for a family-night service at our temple. . . . Rabbi Jimmy is a wonderful, down-to-earth guy who loves . . . hearing about the mystical experiences of others. . . . I pulled Jimmy aside and asked him if he had ever heard the term "Damus." This was all I shared with him. He suddenly took out a pen and started writing in Aramaic and then Hebrew. After pondering over his writings for a moment, he looked up and said, "Sure, Damus or Damas, depending on the spelling, translates to 'messenger of death.' According to our (Jewish) tradition, the messenger of death or angel of death is a positive being who assists the dying. Where did you hear this term? It isn't that common."

I was speechless! I didn't know what to say. My youngest son had been receiving deathbed visions. Suddenly, I started to cry. Rabbi Jimmy found my response somewhat alarming and asked, "What's up?" While blowing my nose, I shared with him about our strange visitor.

His only response was "Wow!" [3]

My father-in-law gently passed away in my husband's arms on Friday the thirteenth, the day after Hanukkah, right after his favorite television program, the 10:00 news. After his death, my young son Josh received no more visitations from Damus.

My husband had great difficulty believing an angel was visiting his son until he, too, encountered a vision from the beyond. Michael had seen his father's pastel spirit begin to leave his dying body, just days before the passing. It was this experience, along with an ADC encounter the day after his father died, that changed him from a stubborn skeptic to an open-minded seeker.

Today, Michael has no doubt an angel visited his three-year-old son. For him, the words of another scientifically minded individual validated that such encounters were not so infrequent. Dr. Melvin Morse, a pediatric physician, has been researching childhood NDEs years. Here is what he had to say about visions of angels.

ॐ In my own research I have found angels to be an integral part of visions of all kinds. At least 50 percent of the children in my studies see "guardian angels" as a part of their near-death experience.[4]

Investigators have also discovered that when children see angels, they aren't always the big-winged, blond-haired, blue-eyed creatures depicted on greeting cards. My son saw an angel who had red hair and looked like a kid. Here is one more narrative involving angels documented by another physician, Sir William Barrett.

ANGELS WITHOUT WINGS

In 1864, a ten-year-old girl named Daisy lay dying from a terrible illness. During her final days, her sister Lulu would sit with her at her bedside. Here is what Daisy told her sister about angels.

"Oh Lulu, is it not strange? We always thought the angels had wings! But it must be a mistake; they don't have any."

Lulu replied, "But they must have wings, else how do they fly down from heaven?" "Oh, but they don't fly," she answered, "They just come . . ."

Once I inquired, "How do you see the angels?" She replied, "I do not see them all the time; but when I do, the walls seem to go away, and I can see ever so far . . ."

"Oh Papa do you hear that? It is the singing of angels. Why you ought to hear it, for the room is full of it, and I can see them, there are so many; I can see them miles and miles away."[5]

I have worked with children for twenty-five years, and rarely have I come across a spiritual tale that was pure, made-up fantasy. There is a difference between childhood fantasy, fabricated for specific purposes, and the reporting of actual events. In assisting those who have been sexually violated, it is extremely important for me to be able to discern fact from fabrication. From time to time, untrue allegations of abuse are used in nasty divorce cases involving child custody. In these sad situations, children can create incidences of abuse to please a particular parent.

The majority of spiritual accounts I have heard from children do not carry with them the pressures, manipulations, or neediness for approval that is contained within other childhood fabrications. When children share spiritual adventures, there is a sense of excitement, purity, and, at times, downright irritation toward the adults who have difficulty hearing about such experiences.

By "hearing" what young voices have to say, we, too, can once again experience the wonder of childhood. In the following account a three-year-old grandchild has a vision, which causes his grandmother to pay attention to what he shares. Notice how detailed this angelic encounter is.

GRANDPA AND THE ANGEL

I was feeding my grandson . . . age three, lunch. He was facing the window in my kitchen, and I was sitting on the left to him and the door was behind me. All of a sudden, he got so excited and started saying with much excitement that "Grandpa" was here. I went to the window and pulled up the blind so that he could see there was no car in the driveway. He continued to eat and did not say anymore.

I walked into the dining room and my grandson got up to follow me. He pulled on my slacks and said, "Grandma, that was your angel." I took him back into the kitchen and sat him down in the chair that he had been sitting on. I cupped his face and looked into his eyes and said, "Tell me again what you just said to me."

He said that there was an angel and that it had Grandpa's eyes. He said it was big and had a lot of colors like blue, green, red, and purple, and he said it was like a rainbow. I then asked him, "Where is it now? Is it still here?" He pointed to the door and said, "That's where it was, but it is not there now." I asked, "Where did it go?" He pointed to the ceiling in my kitchen and said, "Up there, to heaven to God, but Jesus closed the hole [in the ceiling]." My husband died about three weeks later and was not sick. He died suddenly in his sleep. Every time my grandson and I talk about Grandpa, he says, "Oh, Grandpa is up there with Jesus."

Once again, we witness innocence urgently trying to relay an important communication of hope to an older caretaker. This grandmother did listen, and when her beloved husband passed, she took comfort in her grandchild's vision. Had she ignored him, belittled, and dismissed his angelic encounter, she would have missed an opportunity to embrace a spiritual message, one that would ease the sting of eventual grief and loss.

Over the years, I have noticed that with regard to situations involving death and dying, young children seem to have natural access to other realms of reality. When children see angels, deceased relatives, beings of brilliant light, heavenly landscapes, or celestial creatures with red hair, the blow from the passing of a loved one can be lessened. In my practice as a mental-health clinician, I have watched young children unknowingly ease the pain their parents feel over such losses. Here is one of my favorite accounts. This little boy is very assured that his favorite great aunt is just fine.

GREAT AUNT ANTOINETTE'S ANGELS

My Aunt Antoinette, at age seventy-eight . . . was in a nursing home at the time and my sons and I visited regularly. She was particularly close to my youngest son, who was two . . . Tyler Evan and I began to visit her daily first thing in the morning after my two older sons were off to elementary school . . .

Our visits continued daily, and eventually the day came when it was very clear the end had come. Aunt Ann was weak but, as usual, was clearly thrilled to see her Tyler who by now was almost three and a half. Tyler was aware she was very, very sick. He had made a very special friend, Ulysses, who was the maintenance man at the nursing facility. Ulysses would take Tyler to the arts and crafts room so he could visit with the other patients while I sat with my aunt. I prayed, sang hymns, held her, and just loved her.

Weakly, she began telling me who was coming to visit her. All were deceased relatives. I encouraged her to look for the light, that the family would guide her home. Three times during the course of several hours she opened her eyes, looked over my shoulders, over my head, and simply said, "Angel." At the time, I thought she meant I was her angel.

She told me she loved me, my prayers continued, her breathing became more labored, her eyes closed. These were the last words she ever spoke, as she never regained consciousness again.

During these hours I spent with her, Ulysses brought Tyler back into the room every half hour or so, so he could see I was still there with his dearly loved Great Aunt Antoinette. Eventually, it was time for me to take Tyler home and meet my older sons from school. I had planned on going back to the nursing home after getting the boys settled, but the call came that she had passed gently and quietly.

I had to go to the nursing home to sign the authorization for her body to be transported to the funeral parlor. I was quite sad and cried when I told my boys that Great Aunt Ann had died. Tyler, my precious boy, threw his arms around me and said, "Mommy, don't cry. Didn't you see the three angels standing behind you waiting to take Great Aunt Antoinette to heaven?" The grace and peace this gave me was incredible.

He insisted on going to the funeral, insisted he view her body to "be sure she was gone." I was apprehensive but carried him to the casket, and with complete joy, he loudly announced, "Yep, she's gone! See?" He also shared she was at the funeral parlor with the angels. My three-year-old Tyler said Aunt Antoinette was happy and he was not sad, so I shouldn't be either.

Supporting children when they talk about spiritual occurrences is essential. If they sense that we as adults are not open to such things, they will not share with us. Many religious institutions quickly discount otherworldly visions. This, too, can give a child the message that what they are experiencing is wrong or improper.

When my book on deathbed visions was first published, I received numerous e-mails from extreme religious groups accusing me of doing not only the devil's work, but dabbling in black magic! This was most upsetting, but as an adult, I was able to recognize intellectually that such comments were ridiculous. Young children do not have the emotional maturity or self-confidence to make such judgments. If they are told their experiences are bad, mistaken, crazy, silly, demonic, or ridiculous, or if they receive cold silence in response to sharing, they will quickly learn never to discuss such encounters openly. The following accounts make my point perfectly clear.

NO ONE TO TALK TO

Between my junior and senior year in high school, back in 1970, two classmates of mine were out partying. Things ended in tragedy and they were involved in an accident. The driver survived, but the passenger was killed. I was a friend of the passenger, but could not bring myself to attend her funeral with my other classmates. If I didn't attend the funeral, it wasn't real.

Later that summer, I traveled from my home state to another state on a trip with my local Girl Scout troop. We made many stops along the way with our final destination a few days at a state park along the shoreline of Lake ——. Being that it was a warm sunny day, and we were all teenagers, we all spent the day sunbathing on the beach. [The] lake has some of the whitest beaches I've ever seen. The beach was very crowded with many people.

At one point, I looked up and "saw" with my physical eyes, my friend from my high school, who had passed away in that tragic accident, one month prior. She looked absolutely beautiful and whole. Of course, I was always taught that when people died, they were dead. I turned deathly pale. Back in those times, you just didn't tell people you had seen a "ghost." My friends looked at me and asked me what was wrong. They said I looked as though I had just seen a ghost or something. I looked again and the girl was gone. All I could say was, "I think I just did." Of course, they were concerned. They saw nothing.

For this young teen, the above ADC experience had been frightening and she had "known" intuitively not to talk about it. She had been taught that when someone died, they were dead and that was it! Her vision of her childhood friend, after she had passed, ran counter to everything she had been raised to believe about death and dying. Imagine how lonely it was to closet away this experience. Only when she was an adult was she able to fully appreciate it. As a matter of fact, this childhood incident enabled her to heal from a tragic loss later on in adult life. Just think of the healing she could have experienced during her teen years if she had had an open-minded adult to talk to.

Speaking of lonely, in the next example, a young girl's behavior totally confuses her parents. What is so interesting about this account is that it shows how an adult's own spiritual uneasiness can impact children.

A CHILD'S LONELY PREMONITION

When I was about nine, my mother, father, and I went on a family vacation to [a lake]. I suddenly began to have this incredibly sad feeling that my father was going to die. I brooded about it constantly and worried my mother with it. She assured me repeatedly that my father, who was right there with us, was fine and in no danger. Still, the feeling persisted, dark and terribly heavy. Need I add that all this brooding did not make our vacation a barrel of laughs for anyone, especially with me moping around and crying, on and off, every day? I think my parents were getting a little exasperated with me.

About the fourth night of our vacation, we received a telegram that my grandfather, my father's father, was dying in New York State. We threw everything in the car and rushed home . . . so we could pack and get up there. And my feeling of dread lifted immediately. My grandfather did die within a few days. Strangely, my mother, who had had similar experiences herself on at least two occasions, did not relate to what was going on with me. Maybe she just didn't want to freak out a nine-year-old. Whatever her reasons, we never spoke of it again.

What I found fascinating about the above example is that the mother of the child had experienced premonitions of her own. Unfortunately, because the mother obviously had difficulty accepting her own spiritual forewarnings, she was unable to understand her daughter's experience. Chances are the mother of this child had never received assistance or support in accepting her own encounters. As a parent who has experienced deathbed visions, premonitions, and after-death communications, it was essential for me to come to terms personally with these events. Once I did this, I was well prepared not only to listen to my children's spiritual experiences, but also to support them in understanding what they were all about.

In this final account, when it comes to getting a message across to Mom or Dad, we see just how persistent both children and loved ones living in an afterlife existence can be.

MOMMA, GRANDMA REALLY WAS HERE

My three-year-old daughter came to me and said, "Momma, Grandma is here." Thinking my mother-in-law was at the front door, I went to see if it really was her. (My own mother had passed some time ago, so I naturally assumed my daughter wasn't talking about her.) Well, my mother-in-law wasn't at the front door, so I dismissed my daughter's concern. The next day, my daughter came to me again, was pulling on my clothes, and saying, "Momma, Grandma is in the rocking chair."

Walking into the room where the rocking chair was, I saw that it was rocking, so I asked my daughter, "Which grandmother are you talking about?" She replied, "Grandma [Grandmother's name]," who happened to be my deceased mother. Several nights later, my son came to tell me he had had a rather strange dream. He said his grandmother (my deceased mother) had come to him in a dream and that the two of them had had a good talk. He said she looked great, younger than he remembered. He then added, "I asked her if she was going to stay and she said no, that she had to go." She said that besides visiting him [the son], she was here to pick up Grandpa. My father, her husband, and the grandpa my mother spoke about during my son's dream, died three days later.

The innocence of childhood opens the door to other realms of reality. Young minds can "see" what the rest of us have learned to ignore. By following the steps below, not only can we teach our children how to trust these gifts from the beyond, but we, too, can learn to reclaim our own God-given sixth sense. If a child shares otherworldly visions, premonitions, dreams, an NDE, OBE (out-of-body experience, or separation of the soul from the body without a near-death trauma), or any other related encounter:

1. Initially, just listen without interruption or judgment. Do not discount, belittle, or justify what is shared. If you cannot listen, find someone who can.
2. After the child has shared, ask open-ended questions such as, "How did that make you feel?" "What do you think about that?" "Should we find some books or go online to see if we can discover more information about what you experienced?"

3. Have the child draw what they encountered with a box of colored crayons or markers.

A friend of my son's shared with us, in a very off-the-cuff manner, that he had seen a blue "circle thing" floating around his house. After hearing this, I led my son and his friend upstairs to the computer room. We went online and investigated visions of spirits in the form of circular orbs. Much to their delight, we found gobs of sites. "Hey! That's what I saw," announced the little boy!

Later on that day, the mother of the child came to gather up her son. When we showed her the pictures of the orbs, she responded, "My husband said he saw the same thing, but he won't really talk about it." Always remember, out of the mouths of babes can come the validation many of us adults crave.

chapter five

No, I'm Not Hallucinating— Seeing, Hearing, Feeling, and Smelling Is Believing!

"I lay there with the moonlight pouring into the room, through the window, and this mist floating across my bed. Yes, a mist, it sounds like a special effect, but that's what it was."[1]

—Roger Moore, actor

*A*ctor Roger Moore played confident superspy James Bond in seven Hollywood blockbuster movies. While observing a visitor from an afterlife realm, his self-assured, action-hero, tough-guy persona was nowhere to be found! This misty guest appeared not only once, but twice! The following night, Moore's uninvited visitor returned. For this well-known celebrity, believing involved seeing the typically invisible.

When most of us think of reality, we look at the hard, straight-backed chair upon which we sit, the fluffy bed we climb into nightly, the loud radio broadcasting the daily news, and the different flavored foods we put into our mouth to nourish our body. For the majority of us, the belief is if we can't see, taste, hear, or touch it, IT isn't real. If we see beings of light, angels, heavenly sites, or beloved deceased relatives alive and well, with our own physical sight, it can radically alter our fast-held perceptions of what we once considered "true reality" to be.

In recent times, hearing the voices of the departed, receiving messages or premonitions from celestial creatures, tuning into heavenly music, bells, harps, or the flutter of an angel's wings brought out mental-health professionals in crisp white lab coats, with syringes full of powerful anti-psychotic medication. Even though no obvious source is visible, single flower smells, such as roses or lilacs, from a world beyond might tickle our noses, but can we truly trust these experiences?

An otherworldly "drop in" that is revealed by the five senses can wreak havoc on lifelong belief systems. Once confronted with mists of spirit light or a "hello" from a deceased grandparent, we are forced to ask, "If I'm not hallucinating, just what are my senses trying to tell me?" A number of years ago, my own understanding of reality was shaken to the core.

The Ancient Psychomanteum: A Personal Experience with STE Visions

The modern-day apparition chamber, or psychomanteum, is the brainchild of well-known NDE researcher Dr. Raymond Moody, and it is based on the ancient Greek technique of "mirror gazing." The psychomanteum is "an apparition chamber in which a mirror was used in order to bring forth visions of the dead."[2] Moody's book, *Reunions: Visionary Encounters with Departed Loved Ones*, goes into great detail to describe the afterlife visions some experiencers have encountered inside the confines of the contemporary psychomanteum chamber.

Down through the ages, humans have found ways to induce contact with the unseen world. Every civilization on the planet has some sort of historical lore related to calling up dearly departed loved ones. Mirror gazing is just one example of this. Here is what Professor Don Morse, editor-in-chief of *The Journal of Religion and Psychical Research*, had to say about such ancient practices.

> ❧ Ancient methods used to bring forth apparitions include: gazing into crystal balls, cauldrons, bowls, basins, cups, and other vessels filled with liquid; staring into lakes (and other bodies of water); and peering into mirrors. Apparitions have been described in all kinds of cultures since the dawn of history. Biblical prophets such as Ezekiel and the apostle Paul have had apparitions.[3]

I met Moody in the early 1990s, right at the height of his involvement with the psychomanteum. He invited me to come to his home to investigate current-day mirror-gazing practices. Though I was extremely skeptical and did not have a great deal of faith in this ancient device, I decided to take Moody up on his offer. The following is a letter I wrote to a friend of mine, just days after my return home.

WHAT CAN I LEARN FROM THIS?

Though words can never fully describe my experience, I will try to explain to you what I encountered. When I arrived at Moody's, I immediately learned that on the previous night a professional woman, who had recently lost her husband, had had an interesting experience in the psychomanteum. She had made contact with her father, who had passed thirty years ago, and saw him in solid form. He told her to quit worrying about her husband, that he was just fine. Even after hearing her riveting account, I had decided I wasn't going to be having any profound experiences that weekend.

Three psychomanteums were set up around Moody's very eccentric, 100-year-old house. Within these devices, one of which had been built into the house, the walls are completely black. Along with this, there is a mirror hanging on the wall at one end, while at the other, facing the mirror, is a chair. That's it!

During the first day of my visit, I spent about thirty minutes in two of the psychomanteums. Seated comfortably, I reflected on my relationships with those loved ones of mine who had passed, and as I had predicted, nothing out of the ordinary happened. From a historical perspective I found the psychomanteums interesting, but eventually decided enough was enough and spent the rest of the day chatting with other guests.

That evening, I enjoyed a light supper with the rest of Moody's visitors and had a delightful time talking with Dianne Arcangel, who has spent years researching both ancient and modern-day psychomanteums.

While eating dessert, I suddenly had a strong desire to put my plate down and go upstairs to the third psychomanteum. I had not been in this one. What was funny about this sudden "urge" was that during dinner, I made fun of this particular psychomanteum. A rather obsessive engineer had built it.

So, up the stairs I trudged, like a woman on a mission. Into the black box I went and sat down. Within just a few minutes of mirror gazing (just looking into a plain old mirror hanging on a wall, about four feet away) a mist, clouds, or blue-gray "something" started pouring out of the mirror.

A swirl of mist touched me on my right wrist and I became frightened. At this point, Dianne Arcangel happened to be walking by, heard me gasp, and asked if she could help me. I responded with, "I'm glad you are there [just outside the psychomanteum] because it's getting weird in here. I don't know who's visiting, but there are many, and I'm feeling very overwhelmed!" Something intuitively told me I was encountering many visitors from the other side.

Dianne asked me if I wanted to continue. Hearing her voice calmed me down, and I said yes. After she left, I began saying to myself, "What can I learn from this?" over and over again. This mantra kept me grounded. Within moments, it was happening again. This time, the mirror first became black in color and then light. After this, white light tinged in blue started sprinkling down upon me. I wasn't scared, and I could even hear Moody talking on the telephone in the next room. Then the sprinkle of light turned into balls of light. These balls of light started to get bigger, and it looked like they were trying to take form. One began to take the shape of a head, and I thought to myself, "I wonder if that is my grandmother?"

The next part of the experience is still hard to talk about. I get very emotional. One of these bluish-white orbs, not very large in size, hit me on my left side, near my heart area. Though it felt like a light push, it literally took my breath away. It was as if the light had gone through me. With this, I suddenly felt very peaceful, joyous, calm, and intensely loved. I also noticed the temperature in the psychomanteum was suddenly cooler.

Then I saw more light around me and I was inundated with unlimited unconditional love. Because it felt as though things were happening rather quickly, I sensed urgency for contact from whoever was reaching out to me. With this awareness, very thin etheric streams of whirling white energy came toward my left side, touching my left arm, as if in an embrace. From this soft, cool touch, I felt pure amazement and joy.

I will never know what would have happened next because one of Moody's more aggressive visitors suddenly burst in and told me he wanted to try this psychomanteum. With this intrusion, the swirling, loving light immediately disappeared. For a moment, I just sat there stunned. Then, in a state of awe, love, confusion, grief, and numbness, I got out of the psychomanteum and started to talk to the other guest about my experience, but then silenced myself. Outside the room, I once again found Dianne Arcangel. After seeing the look on my face, she led me to an outside porch where I began to cry. The encounter had overwhelmed me and I now found myself missing the loving touch I had received from the cool, swirling whitish-blue light.

Out of a group of approximately ten or so participants, I was one of two who experienced a reunion. My rational mind wants to explain the experience away, but it can't. I saw with my eyes and tactilely felt something beyond this physical plane of existence. During the encounter, my intuition was certain, unshakable. The overpouring of gray misty clouds that initially floated toward me, the whitish-blue balls or orbs of soft, love energy and light that entered me, the unexpected drop in temperature inside the psychomanteum, and the streams of pure white, swirling thin light, energy that came toward me, encircling me, cannot be explained away. I am changed forever.

When I have shared this dramatic experience with skeptics, I am met with a number of questions such as, "Had you been drinking?" "Were you on drugs?" "Was the mirror rigged?" "Who was flashing a flashlight at you?" and "Were you psychologically stressed at the time?"

"I don't drink, nor do I do drugs, and I'm boringly sane" is the response I typically begin with. Having examined the mirrors hanging in the psychomanteum, I can attest to the fact that there were no secret lights or hidden panels contained within them. They were typical mirrors.

As I said earlier, words cannot fully describe the experience I encountered in the psychomanteum. After returning home, "dazed and confused," I found myself integrating this new spiritual encounter. For about six months I felt like the "Energizer Bunny," experienced mood swings, and a buzzing sensation. Recently departed friends were coming by to "chat" with me, to share their first impressions of the afterlife. I had four visits from deceased loved ones within a month's time. Because the experience was so life altering, it took me months even to share the full extent of the encounter with caring, supportive friends. This was a mistake.

Because these afterlife encounters were very spontaneous, the first few were most unnerving. It was as if my psychomanteum encounter had opened up some psychic door, and for a short period of time, this invisible entryway remained ajar. After a third encounter with one more deceased loved one, I found myself asking, "How come this is happening?"

Like Roger Moore, bedtime became an unpredictable time. After my psychomanteum experience, a multitude of spontaneous nighttime visions created even more confusion and concern for me. Drifting off to sleep, I would catch a glimpse of a passing spirit, then sit straight up in bed and wonder, "Will this ever stop?!"

It is important for STE-ers to understand that after the earthquake, there can be a number of aftershocks. A powerful

STE encounter can open us up to additional experiences with the unseen world. Because of this, it is essential to find a trusted friend, family member, religious guide, or mentor with whom to talk about this.

For me, the psychomanteum provided my first contact with visions. Though the earthquake was strong, the aftershocks proved to be even more confusing. If I had grabbed on to someone who could have heard what I had to share about this experience, I strongly suspect I would have saved myself a great deal of confusion.

Many STE visions can occur at bedtime. Before we move on, let's investigate nighttime STEs just a bit more.

Bedtime—a Ticket to an STE Encounter

One does not need to be ill or near death to have STEs. One does not need to be an expert at meditation to reach a trance state, and visions of the unusual can spontaneously visit when we least expect them. Though my one experience with mirror gazing induced months of nighttime visions, all our Hollywood James Bond superhero needed to do was ready himself for bed. While he was in a light trance state, preparing for sleep, his otherworldly houseguest suddenly popped in. The following night, the famous actor was visited again. Perhaps you, too, have encountered an unusual otherworldly bedtime vision, STE encounter, spiritual awakening, or strange dream. Know you and James Bond have something in common and that such experiences are not that unusual.

The hypnagogic or light trance, a state of mind related directly to out-of-body experiences, after-death communications, and premonitions, occurs naturally just before we slip off into dreamland. This is the most common entrance into the unseen world. During this twilight time, while relaxed and on the verge of sleep, the hypnagogic state takes over and vivid visions can occur. During such moments it's as if we have one foot in this reality and the other somewhere else. Here is an excellent example of spontaneous contact with a once-unseen reality, just before drifting off to sleep.

I DIDN'T EXPECT THIS!

I always felt "different" and I never had much to say because my thinking seemed out of line with everyone else's. In retrospect, I can see now that there were signs all along the way leading up to my powerful spiritual experience. I had survived numerous life difficulties, including several painful relationships.

Then there was the "almost" mastectomy. In 1982, I went into the hospital and signed for a double radical mastectomy. Upon returning to consciousness in the recovery room, a nurse was slapping my face and hollering, "Wake up, Janet. You don't have cancer!" Was it spontaneous healing? With what I have learned about healing I can see why that might happen. Needless to say, I was elated! After that, I took conscious steps to begin changing my life.

In 1986, I got mononucleosis and the doctor told me I wouldn't get better, that it would keep recurring. It was then I started exploring holistic health. The mono has not returned. The meditation, tai chi kung, Reiki training, and other self-healing lifestyle changes stirred up lots of old unresolved trauma, and I was forced to clean this up, too.

My experience involved a spontaneous Kundalini awakening in 1996. Prior to this, I had no knowledge of such experiences. I'd just gone to bed and there was suddenly the classic great swooshes of energy. There was so much love! Words cannot adequately describe what I felt. It enveloped me—a connection with the Divine. Then came the intense realization of unity, that we are all interconnected, that everything is as it is supposed to be. But, with this overwhelming sense of love came a price tag. I had major problems on all levels. Physically, for some time I had pains in my head, and I thought something was wrong with my heart. There were other pains, and I felt as though I couldn't get grounded. Along with this, I was emotionally overwhelmed for nearly four months. Spiritually, just about everything was confusing!

At the time I didn't have a vocabulary to know what to call these happenings. It took me a long time to get used to this kind of thing, telepathy, precognition, voices (mentally perceived), connection with Spirit as guide, incidents of channeling, or maybe it is abstract intuition.

Interestingly, divine synchronicity kicked in. I turned on TV and saw a program on Kundalini featuring a medical doctor who understood just what I was experiencing. I jumped on the phone, contacted her, and she referred me to a wonderful transpersonal therapist. He was amazing. This man carefully guided me through the confusion my spiritual awakening had created for me. I am so grateful to him, and I am grateful to the wonderful doctor who was there to help me to understand the responses a Kundalini awakening can produce.

I tell my story because I keep suggesting others tell theirs. If everyone who has had an NDE or STE talks and writes about their experiences, they will stop seeming to be "kooky" and will be accepted more as a normal process, and one with the most amazing potential!

Janet's story is a classic example of a spontaneous STE. She climbs into bed, and boom! A spontaneous Kundalini experience occurs. As we dig deeper into her story, we do learn that Janet had begun taking better care of herself, healing old grief and loss, reducing stress, exercising, and using alternative means such as herbs and meditation to improve her physical, psychological, and spiritual state of being. Next thing she knows she's having a full-blown STE!

In the first chapter I described how I had induced an STE with Kundalini meditation. If you remember, I, too, encountered a number of physical, emotional, and spiritual consequences to this. Unlike myself, Janet didn't go "looking" for an intense spiritual adventure, but nevertheless the experience found her and changed the course of her life forever.

Today, she is the coordinator for an organization dedicated to assisting individuals in need of assistance after having out-of-body experiences, Kundalini awakenings, near-death experiences, or other altered states of consciousness. Spiritual Emergence Service comes to us from Canada, and the organization provides therapists for clients who have had such experiences.

Janet is not alone when she describes the interconnectedness she felt with the Divine. Feeling encircled in unconditional love and joined with the universe seems to be a common theme reported by those who have had STEs. To understand just what I mean, read the next account.

ENLIGHTENMENT ON THE CAUSEWAY

It had been a long day. Wednesday was severe trauma day at the office. Clients recovering from abuse and sexual damage had ruled the morning. That afternoon had belonged to a woman who had been raised in the Ku Klux Klan, and the elderly grandmother who, during WWII, at the age of four, had jumped over dead bodies in East Germany while escaping the invading Communists. Driving home I felt exhausted and began asking, "Why me? Why was I chosen to assist those who had witnessed and survived the unspeakable terror hidden within the underbelly of humanity?" I was feeling very oppressed and heavy as my car began to creep onto a causeway, linking the mainland to the small island I live on.

As I reached the top of the causeway, a strange lightness pushed my sad sense of heaviness aside, and I was suddenly overtaken by a powerful consciousness. Looking at the sea, I began to feel as though my body had no end. I felt connected to the turquoise sea beneath the causeway, the grasses, trees, and flowers growing near the water's edge, the other cars flying past me with their many different drivers, the multitude of fish in the ocean, the dolphins diving into the deep, birds flying over head, and the fading blue sky with its emerging stars and moon.

At that moment, I "felt" within my being and knew "intuitively" that we were all one. My sense of separation had evaporated. There was no beginning, no end. It was as if streams of energy making up my essence were intertwined with all that was around me. There were no divisions. There was no right, nor was there wrong, no good, no bad, no better, no less than. It just was!

I was inundated with intense emotion and awareness and found myself having difficulty driving. The joy that accompanied total understanding of the true meaning of life was indescribable. Words are not enough. The meaning of my life, of life in general, became crystal clear and I found myself laughing out loud.

This moment of enlightenment on the causeway is an STE I had several years ago. Out of the blue, pure love wrapped itself around me and I felt connected to the infinite. And, as other STE-ers have shared, words cannot fully express just what it was I felt at that instant. It is also important to note that I had done nothing to induce this specific experience.

Interestingly, like Janet, I had been clearing out some past emotional grief and loss. Along with this, I had recently changed my diet and was practicing yoga on a regular basis. In reviewing accounts of this nature, I am finding there appears to be a strong connection between healing the self, physically, emotionally, and spiritually, and STEs. The following story once again hints at a connection between initial self-healing and eventual STE encounters. Abandoned at eight months of age and suffering from agoraphobia, this brave woman wades through the rubble of her past and unexpectedly receives the joy of healing.

TRUE LIBERATION

For several years prior to my STE I had many struggles, which I eventually overcame. Gone was the depression and night terrors I had suffered . . . I was taking good care of myself by meditating, exercising, and generally relishing my newfound freedom. Little did I know that I was about to experience "True Liberation."

I had been meditating every afternoon for the last year and a half. On one particularly lovely spring day, I arose with the calmness and peace associated with a lengthy meditative state. I went downstairs to my living room, and I noticed as I looked out the window that I was ONE with the blades of grass and the rocks in the road. I was enveloped in a LOVE I could not put into words. This DIVINE LOVE was in everything and in me. At the core of my being was this LOVE as it was in everyone else.

In this state, which I refer to as a state of grace, there was no right or wrong, no good or bad, no judgment whatsoever. Fear was nonexistent! There was no death and I knew that we all lived forever. Everyone I met was LOVE. It did not matter what they looked like, behaved like. I was them and they were me. We were all connected. The utter joy is indescribable. I knew we did not end at our fingertips. The peace and bliss are beyond words. I became aware that a PRESENCE other than what I usually think of as myself was looking through my eyes. I had become ONE with this INFINITE AWARENESS, which simply sees without judgment. It is the very essence of life, eternal life. I wanted nothing, needed nothing. It was a peace that is indescribable. . . . To know that we are all connected in spirit and to have witnessed the ONENESS of all creation in a state of LOVE and Bliss is to glimpse God.[4]

Helen ends her tale by adding that the human language can never fully do justice to her experience. Like the previous accounts, Helen had also learned to use meditation to clear her mind, relax, and improve her sense of spiritual well-being.

There are many different types of meditation. I have already mentioned Kundalini meditation. Most methods of meditation can produce an intense state of relaxation. Finding one that works for you is the key to successful meditation. Sitting comfortably, clearing the mind, and gazing into the flame of a candle are simple steps you can take toward beginning the practice of meditation. After spending time experimenting with this form of relaxation, you might want to read up on various other forms of meditation. A friend of mine did just this.

TOP OF MY HEAD BLEW OFF!

Bill graduated with a degree in engineering from Rutgers, taught college, and had his own successful business. As he says, "I had a scientific education and seemed to be analytical by nature." Life challenges led him to begin practicing Zen Buddhist meditation. After years of practice, he had a very unexpected, powerful awakening. Here, he describes what his STE felt like.

[It felt like] the top of my head blew off. I felt as though a river of light and glorious emotion was racing down through me with the force of a fire hose. It knocked me down. I lay on the floor in total awe. For several minutes, the brain did not think, the body did not move. I could only experience the amazing feeling and light flowing through me. It is impossible to exaggerate the intensity of the feeling . . .

After several minutes of light and glorious feeling, my being began to settle down to a state of extreme bliss. Then I started to see the history of my life go by. My emotional state now was one of unconditional love. My mental state was, "This life has been exactly the way it was supposed to be."

After that, I started to see magnificent displays of knowledge. I had understanding of things in ways we just don't possess in our everyday lives. That's why it is so very hard to describe these episodes . . .

Then I felt a slight physical jolt. My attention moved around inside myself to see what that was. Immediately, I knew that all fear of death had just left . . .

For five or six months after, it did look as though it was all going to be gravy; I was in a state of bliss day and night. One time, months later, I was just sitting, enjoying my bliss, when even higher feelings started to roll over me. I started to see faces going by, people I knew, some well, some not so well. Again, the only possible state was awe. Shortly [after, my] brain said, "Wow. What's this? What's this? What's this?" After a little while, a word appeared in consciousness. The word was forgiveness. Apparently, I had forgiven all those people.[5]

Today, Bill runs a support group for near-death experiencers in Houston, Texas. Glimpsing other realities can create a "psychic" shift within us. Our priorities can change from being "materially focused," amassing more money, power, recognition, or material possessions, to being "people or planet oriented," with a desire to be of service. After a powerful STE, the banker who was once consumed with increasing his pocketbook suddenly makes a career change and becomes a mental-healthcare worker. A woman who spent years questing for more professional recognition and control chucks it all for the life of an artist after having a profound mystical experience. These are not uncommon scenarios.

Before his intense spiritual awakening, the man in the following account had been practicing Hatha Yoga for some time. When people in the United States talk about yoga, they may unknowingly be referring to Hatha Yoga. This yoga discipline is the most popular form of yoga practiced in Western culture. Using body postures, breathing, and meditation, the goal of Hatha Yoga is to increase not only physical well-being, but also emotional serenity and spiritual peace. Five years of yoga practice and intense meditation produced an STE that defined Mark Seelig's path for life. Living in a castle, located deep in a wooded forest in Germany, Dr. Seelig's incredible awakening is as follows.

BLISS AND ECSTASY

The experience occurred on November 11, 1983 . . . I had been practicing Hatha Yoga for approximately five years prior to the experience . . . On the day it happened, I had, as usual, spent several hours doing exercises from the Hatha Yoga tradition, combined with special breathing techniques, followed by extensive sitting periods [Zen meditation].

[Without warning] arousal of the Kundalini tingling and burning sensations [began] moving from the coccyx [tailbone] up the spine . . . [this was followed by] involuntary and violent movements of the body, shaking of the spine, sudden outburst of tears and laughter, visions of colors, and explosive lights inside my skull, auditory phenomena . . . I was not able to sit any more, and so I got up to move around and soon felt the urge to be out in nature.

At that time, I lived in an old castle in the middle of the woods in Germany . . . As the sensations became more pronounced . . . I discontinued my sitting meditation, got up and went outside into the forest . . . out among the trees the phenomena became even more powerful. I had tears of joy about the beauty of nature, about the fact that I was existing . . . as I walked through the fresh air in the middle of the night, I saw white and purple light balls exploding, I heard voices, and I "saw" people I used to feel resentment toward, only to realize that now I had pure compassion and love for them.

After feeling five hours of intense energy, bliss, and ecstasy, the sensations began to lessen.

The following day, Dr. Seelig had what he describes as a deliberately induced out-of-body experience or OBE. This particular OBE has many of the characteristics similar to a near-death experience or NDE. The only difference is, he was not physically near death. For this reason, Dr. Seelig refers to it as a "near-life experience." Though it was not his intention to experience an OBE, he believes that his STE awakening the previous evening was responsible for the out-of-body encounter he had the following day.

> I had the feeling of flying and the bliss I felt was so unsurpassable that I never wanted to come back to my body . . . Returning to the body seemed like death to me. I went through a tunnel. I saw entities that felt to be deceased relatives, speaking to me in a "wordless language." At the end of the tunnel, I encountered a light being which seemed to come from beyond. The being started alerting me in the most loving way . . . that I had not yet finished with life in the body . . . under extreme feelings of regret and sorrow, I decided to return to the body . . . I went back through the tunnel . . . into the physical abode I had left behind. I felt extreme pain and a sense of incredible loss. At the same time, I was filled with utter gratitude for what had been shown and revealed to me. It was clear that my task would now be to move into the integration phase of this experience, and into somehow building life around a spiritual path even more than before . . . Needless to say, the above described experiences have completely shattered my outlook on life, consciousness, religion . . . After my experiences, however, I had proof . . . and I knew for a fact that our entire understanding of who we are is very limited.[6]

After his encounter, Mark Seelig completed academic studies in both psychology and theology and received his Ph.D. from the University of Frankfurt/Main. He then taught at the university for several years. Today, Dr. Seelig is a transpersonal psychotherapist who continues to investigate different states of consciousness.

When one experiences an STE, it is not uncommon to recognize that death is nothing to fear. With this new awareness, certain religious dogma is then discarded and many of society's institutions, biases, prejudices, and obsessions seem irrelevant and even petty. Because these psychological changes happen so quickly and new consciousness is so profound, there can be a sense of depression. Feelings alienated from everyday life often cause experiencers to isolate from family, friends, and co-workers. Finding support and validation for our experiences can help us to move from feeling unique and confused to excited about a new path. The prospect of discovering what this lesson called life has yet to teach can fill us with a fresh sense of adventure.

If your five senses have revealed to you a world beyond current understanding, know you do not have to stand alone. The mystical experience must be shared. But knowing just who to share with makes all the difference in the world. I hope that in sharing several of my own, as well as others', spontaneous STEs with you in this chapter, you are truly beginning to see that you are not on your own. Know that you will be given the tools necessary to establish a community of like-minded people with whom to share your encounters. Talking safely about STE adventures can begin.

chapter six

Our Furry Friends—
Special STE Encounters

"The soul is the same in all living creatures,
although the body each is different."

—Hippocrates, known as the "Father of Medicine" (c. 460 to c. 377 B.C.)

One can't investigate the spiritually transformative experiences of everyday people without hearing about animals. Over the years, numerous people from all walks of life have shared fantastic, otherworldly adventures involving animals with me.

When my book on deathbed visions hit the bookshelves, naturally, family members across the states were excited to see these otherworldly accounts made public. Every time a family gathering took place, someone invariably pulled me aside and said, "Have you got a moment? Do I ever have an interesting tale to share with you!"

A couple of winters ago, Michael, the boys, and I decided to visit relatives living in Nebraska. On this trip, I brought several pounds of fresh, Gulf Coast shrimp. Living by the sea, my family and I are surrounded by unlimited quantities of delectable seafood. We are definitely spoiled. One of the relatives we were to visit had requested a shrimp or two, because in his neck of the woods, seafood consisted of frozen fish that tasted like shoe leather. So, I dutifully stuffed four freshly frozen pounds of large shelled shrimp into my suitcase.

Once we arrived at our destination, there was a blizzard raging outside, but in spite of this, it was time for a good old-fashioned shrimp boil. As I dumped the shrimp into the scalding, seasoned water, one of my husband's relatives, Mona, came into the kitchen and asked if she could help. I could see something was bothering her. While we began preparing a salad, she quietly shared with me her grief about the recent loss of her beloved chocolate retriever. Mona is British, extremely polite, and very sensible, so I was quite surprised by what she had to say.

MY PUP

Our pup had been looking a little ill for sometime. We didn't think it was serious, but decided to take him to the vet just the same. My husband had piled him into the truck and off they had gone. I thought for sure I'd see my pup in a few hours. Later on that day, I decided to sit with a cup of tea. As I sipped my tea, I picked up the newspaper and began reading. While perusing the latest local news, I felt my pup brush up against my leg. He did this often and I responded as usual. I reached down to stroke his beautiful fir.

Absentmindedly, my hand went looking for him while I read the paper. When there was no touch of fur, I remembered he was at the vet's office. Looking up at the clock, I noted it was 2:00 in the afternoon. "Well, isn't that odd?" I thought to myself, and then I went back to my paper.

Approximately thirty minutes later, the vet called. "I'm so

sorry, Mona," the vet began. "There really was nothing I could do. I had to put him to sleep." Unbeknown to us, our pup had been very sick. I was devastated. After drying up my tears I asked, "At what time did you put him to sleep?" With this, the vet replied, "At about two this afternoon."

I was stunned. My pup had left this world at about the time I had felt him brush up against me.

Mona had a pre-death experience with her beloved pet. Her experience with her pup is similar to other deathbed visions I have collected. As I explained earlier, when my own mother died, I was asleep at home, but I felt her presence pass near me.

Did Mona's chocolate retriever stop by to say a similar final farewell? The only difference between my account and that of Mona's is that her otherworldly visitor had fur. Other than that, the accounts are very similar.

The next animal account comes to us from South Africa. With one exception, the following after-death communication has all the characteristics of a classic encounter of its type. With this ADC, not only is the visitation from an animal, but also, the pink creature in discussion is not a typical domesticated pet!

A THANK-YOU FROM A RUNT

I am an animal lover and I had a wonderful experience that I want to share. It happened about six years ago. I arrived at our small holding where my husband kept the pigs. Our sow had had a litter, and among them was a runt. As I approached, a staff member was about to fling the runt into the bush. I stopped him, took the runt, and saw that it was still alive. . . . It was wintertime and I put a heater next to my bed and made a cozy bed for my "baby." My husband shook his head and said it wouldn't survive.

I fed the runt every three hours . . . by three in the morning he woke me up squealing for more formula. I really thought he was going to pull through. . . . The next morning I could see he was weakening and my heart sank. By about 3:00 in the afternoon I could see he was dying.

[After he passed] I cried bitterly. I got my son to dig a hole in the garden, put him in a box, buried him, and said a prayer. That night as I was sinking into sleep, I saw him right in front of me. He pressed his little nose right against my face and I could feel pressure against my cheek. . . . I knew he had come to say thank you.

I don't tell people about this unique experience because they will think I'm crazy. It goes to show you that animals do survive death. Nobody will convince me otherwise.

With a typical ADC experience, there is a visitation from someone special after that loved one has passed on. The above example is no exception. This specific type of encounter is referred to as a tactile ADC, feeling the touch of a deceased loved one. The following is what my friend Professor Morse had to say about such ADCs.

     ∾ After-Death Contacts have involved virtually all of the senses. With tactile ADC, the person feels the touch of the deceased without actually seeing or hearing him/her.[1]

For years, I was skeptical of otherworldly accounts involving animals. Being an animal fan, I had always had a menagerie of fury, feathered, and even scaly creatures around the house. When one of these pets would pass, I would grieve terribly, but then I would remember what society had taught me. Educational and religious institutions had drilled into me that animals were not like humans. As a youth, I had been convinced that only we two-legged mammals had intelligence and souls.

Over the years, I began to question this. My pets had personalities, likes, dislikes, moods, and behaviors peculiar only to them. As time went on, like Hippocrates, I, too, began to believe that "The soul is the same in all living creatures, although the body each is different." An otherworldly encounter with an old cat named Sweetie Pie sealed my belief that animals are spiritual creatures, too.

AN INTERESTING VISITOR

The night was cold and rainy, but it was time to let Broadway, my giant, all paws, golden retriever, out the door for one last time. Before I even turned the doorknob, I heard this scraggly, mournful meow. Standing on my front porch was a bag of bones covered in tufts of orange fur. Upon seeing the dripping wet cat, Broadway made a beeline for the back of the house. He always had been a big baby.

Meowing up a storm, the skinny creature walked over my threshold, as if she owned the place. She then headed straight for a food bowl belonging to our resident fluff ball, Tom. After a few bites, this uninvited guest climbed up onto a blanket lying across the couch and fell fast asleep.

After taking her to the vet, it was determined she was probably on her "last cat" leg, but we decided to care for her as long as she needed us to. Because this animal was such a grouch, my boys named her Sweetie Pie. This cantankerous creature lived with us for the next three years, and she became my favorite pet.

Eventually, my beloved cat's life was coming to an end. As Sweetie Pie lay panting on the cool tiled floor of the downstairs bathroom, I could see she was suffering terribly. My sister Lila had come to the house for a Sunday night fish fry. Typically, when I cooked seafood, Sweetie Pie would be at my feet, pawing my leg, begging for a morsel of seafood delight. But, that was not the case on this evening. I knew in my gut that my fury friend needed to be released from her physical pain, but all vets' offices on the island were closed.

Both my sister and I had studied herbal medicine for years. After sitting with Sweetie Pie for several hours, we knew action had to be taken. The poor thing was burning up with fever, barely breathing, and in obvious agony. Between Lila and I, we put together an herbal concoction that would end Sweetie Pie's terrible pain. Lila then gently held her head, while I administered several droppers of the potent herbs. In minutes, her agony was no more, and I broke down sobbing.

As I ended Sweetie Pie's life, another friend, visiting for the fish fry, had been sitting in the living room. After an hour or so of tears, I wrapped my beloved pet's emaciated body in a towel and came out of the bathroom. My friend was sitting nervously on a chair in the living room, just outside the bathroom. "I have something to tell you," he said. "You might think I'm nuts, but I know what I saw," he added.

"I sat out here the whole time you were in the bathroom with that cat, and as the end drew near, I saw something so very strange. A light, bluish-white light traveled across the living room, toward the bathroom, and then it disappeared. It wasn't a streetlight; how can I describe it? It was like a light with purpose, even intelligence. While it traveled toward the bathroom, I had the sudden impression that this was the spirit of a previous owner coming to get the spirit of that cat. Now where did that idea come from? I have never had a thought even similar to that in my entire life!"

My dear friend is not religious, nor had he ever read anything on NDEs, DBVs, ADCs, psychics, ESP, or spirits. He is a true Texas, meat-and-mashed-potatoes skeptic, a man of concrete science. To this day, with regard to this event, this cautious man refuses to allow me to share his identity with anyone. His fear of ridicule is overwhelming.

Did a deceased previous owner come for the soul of my beloved pet? My once-skeptical friend is convinced of this. Such spiritually transformative encounters beg us to ask, do our pets go to an afterlife existence? Can animals perceive other realities of existence? Do our fury and feathered friends have souls? Are our pets more sensitive to visitors from the other side? Should we be paying more attention to the connections our animal friends have with other realities?

A Little History

In past times, animals were seen as magical creatures that had access not only to this world, but also other worlds to come. How many of us are aware that during the sixteenth century, the Christian Church in England persecuted sweet, fluffy kitty cats? These church fathers believed cats were demons from hell! Until the nineteenth century, our feline friends were closely associated with the occult and witchcraft. Centuries before this in Egypt, the cat was actually worshipped as a god. Killing "Fluffy" was punishable by death. The ancient Egyptians believed cats possessed magical, supernatural abilities. Two of the most popular Egyptian deities were lion-headed Sekhmet, goddess of death, rebirth, and wisdom, and feline-headed Bast, goddess of truth, enlightenment, and sexuality. Egyptian tombs and graves were often full of mummified cats. At the British Museum in London, my family and I noticed mummified cats outnumbered the mummified people! Do our feline friends sense what we typically cannot see, hear, or touch?

KITTY HEARS A VOICE

My beautiful sister . . . died in June at the age of forty-six, after a brief battle with breast cancer. [Before passing] she had at least two out-of-body experiences. I heard her voice early one morning in my house, and as she spoke my cat put his ears back, so I know it was real. Her voice echoed in the hallway. My Mom also heard my sister call her name.

When my family and I first moved into the 100-year-old house that is now our home, we would often smell the strong sent of lilacs in certain rooms. The scent would materialize out of nowhere, and when it did, my cats, with ears pulled back, would spit and hiss. My oldest son even went so far as to pick up one of our kitties and dropped him directly in the midst of the lilac scent. That fur ball bolted out of the room as fast as his little legs could carry him. I believe cats can sense other realities.

AN OMEN FROM MY KITTY

My beloved grandfather died . . . while in the hospital. [Before he passed] I suddenly became very ill with symptoms that were unlike any I had experienced. My cat, who is usually very quiet and docile, was yowling and doing half circles around my chair. I called the hospital and was told they "were working" on my grandfather. Suddenly, my symptoms stopped and my cat went back to normal. Approximately a half-hour later, the hospital called to tell me my grandfather had passed. His time of death occurred at the same time my illness stopped.

Over the years, I have collected many "Empathetic Death-bed Visions." With this type of encounter, a loved one, typically several miles away, physically experiences the death of the one dying. One woman reported to me that she was suddenly hit with terrible pain in her chest area. Not long after this, she received a phone call from a neighbor telling her that her mother had just died of a heart attack. This is not an unusual pre-death experience. The woman in the above account experienced sudden physical illness, while unknown to her, in a hospital, her grandfather was passing. At this same time, her cat was acting very strangely.

Was her cat also sensing her grandfather's departure? Is there more to the animal psyche than we know? If cats have souls, can they not only sense an upcoming passing, but return for a visit once they, too, have left this earth? Like humans, are they capable of experiencing near-death or out-of-body experience? Seeing is believing, and here is a wonderful account from Art Myers, author of *Communicating with Animals: The Spiritual Connection Between People and Animals*.

CATS WHO FLY

Folklore has it that cats are mysterious. I don't know if they're any more mysterious than the rest of us, but I once knew a cat in Lenox, Massachusetts, who had some pretty clever psychic tricks.

For one thing, he lived well past the age of twenty, which is pretty long for a cat to hang around this plane. His name was Michael, and he lived with the Librizzi family.

When Michael was twenty, he did something uncharacteristic—he got sick. They took him to a veterinarian in the next town, who wanted to keep him overnight. It was the first time Michael had ever been away from the family.

That evening, the Librizzis went to a movie. When they returned, they stood on the porch while the elder Terry fished around in her handbag for the house key. Suddenly they saw Michael jump up on the porch, and as Terry opened the door, he ran inside. This was standard procedure. Michael would go for a nightly stroll, then come back and run inside to grab a snack from his dish in the kitchen.

Automatically, Terry opened the door and let Michael in. Then the Librizzis stared at each other. Wasn't Michael at the vet's down in Stockbridge, six miles away? They ran inside, and there was no Michael in sight. They called the vet's office and were told that Michael was still crouched morosely in the cage he'd been put in that afternoon.[2]

The author goes on to say that this entire family was very open to atypical spiritual experiences, so seeing their beloved Michael's spirit, while his physical body lay in a cage at the vet, was startling, but not baffling. Modern science might suggest the family was delusional, superstitious, or overly imaginative. Because of this, it is important to add that the mother of this family was a well-respected university professor of philosophy.

A Little More History

Cats are not the only animals capable of soul journeys. Dogs also have a regal, magical history. The god Anubis had the head of a dog or jackal and the body of a man. Like the cat, this dog-headed God was also worshipped in Egypt. The ancient Egyptians believed Anubis escorted the souls of the dead to their final judgment. Down through the ages, dogs were thought to have a second sight, and it was believed they could see spirits of the deceased. For centuries, there has been a universal idea that dogs can sense an imminent death.

To hear a dog mournfully howl has long been seen as an omen forecasting an upcoming passing. This ability to predict death has often been attributed to the dog's keen sense of smell. As physical death draws near, there are chemical transformations taking place in the body. Do dogs only sense these physical changes? If this is so, why did Abraham Lincoln's dog begin howling and running in circles at the White House just moments before the president was assassinated, some distance away, at a theater? In modern times, as a death draws near, dogs continue to baffle us with their sixth sense. Read the following account. The vision of a deceased pet foretells an upcoming passing. Interestingly, the account comes from a healthcare worker.

GET THAT DOG OUT OF HERE!

I am a nurse and work with terminally ill cancer patients. One particular patient was very close to passing. As I was doing my first rounds of the night, I heard her screaming. When I entered her room, she was saying, "Get that dog out of here!" As I sat on the edge of the bed, I held her hand and asked her what was scaring her so terribly. She replied, "Don't you see?

Don't you see that black poodle, standing in the doorway, staring at me?" Of course, no, I didn't see it, but as we talked she told me of her childhood pet who was a black poodle. When I asked, "Did the dog go to heaven?" she replied, "Yes, a long time ago." I truly believe that this is her childhood poodle, preparing her for her journey home.

Before a passing, visitations from deceased loved ones are not uncommon. With a pre-death vision, it is believed that those who have already made the trip to the afterlife return to prepare a dying loved one for their departure. Is the above account a typical pre-death experience? Yes! The only difference is this visiting spirit has fur, paws, and floppy ears! Below is one other DBV or pre-death experience involving a treasured pet.

MIKKI THE MALTESE DOG

My mother died a few years ago . . . She was not a "religious" person so to speak. However, during her last few weeks of life, she had several visions or contacts with the other side.

She was at her house when we visited her and she talked to us as usual. However, she kept looking out the window onto the front porch. Then, in the middle of our regular conversation, she asked me to tell the girl on the porch to come inside. We looked outside, even though we knew no one was there. . . . I asked her [mother] if she [the girl] was still there, and she said "yes." I never even pretended to let the girl in, but about five minutes later, Mother looked at a spot on the couch next to me and said that the girl was sitting there and she had a baby in her arms. So, I asked my mother what the girl looked like. She said the girl was about eighteen years of age and medium complexion (we are African-American). I was not really perplexed because I believed that she saw her. The ironic thing was that we would go back to normal conversation.

The next day when we were visiting her, my mother told me that the girl was not holding a baby, but a deceased Maltese dog she had named "Mikki." I just said, "Really?" She said, "Yes." I was truly amazed, not scared, not thinking she was out of her mind, none of that, just amazed.

In this example, the daughter goes on to say her mother was on very little pain medication. Notice how similar the above two pre-death visions are. Before passing, each of the dying was visited by a deceased dog that at one time had been a beloved companion.

Our canine friends can also be found in after-death communications. This wonderfully sweet account comes from a child. The STEs of children are chock full of innocence and awe. This one is no exception.

THE COON DOG

My dad died six years ago last February. . . . About three days before he died, he looked up toward the ceiling and remarked that he needed to run after and catch his sister Doris. Doris had passed about two years before Dad did. . . . My dad passed on the same day his youngest brother had passed, four years before. My daughter was awakened one night three or four weeks after Dad had died, and she claimed Grandpa (Dad) was at the bottom of her bed with a Coon dog, and they were both looking at her as she slept.

Visitations from the deceased often occur at nighttime. Departed loved ones seem to know that a visit to grieving loved ones will ease the pain of loss. With this account, it looks like Grandpa is once again side by side with his "Coon dog."

While collecting STEs, I began putting together a file on visions of an afterlife existence. Much to my surprise, I found I had received numerous accounts describing other spiritual domains, which included animals. One very detailed account involves a near-death experience. Jan Price, the author of *The Other Side of Death*, suffered a full heart arrest and suddenly found herself outside of her body. Her NDE tale is riveting, and I strongly suggest you investigate her book. For now, let's look at her encounter with her dear dog, Maggi.

MAGGI AND HEAVEN

. . . I felt that I was being lifted to another level of awareness—and then I found myself in surroundings that appeared to be more substantial—Maggi was there. My beautiful dog, my beloved Springer, came to me. She had died less than a month before, and John and I still ached from her absence.

I felt her presence, her love, and she appeared to me as she had when she was in physical form—only younger, more vital. She said, "You know that Daddy can't handle both of us being gone right now."

"Yes, I'm going back," I replied. . . .

If you are having difficulty accepting the idea that my first encounter on the other side was with a dog, you aren't the only one. While John thought it perfectly natural, one of our daughters became a little upset when I told her about it. I think she would have preferred that her mother be greeted by Jesus, an angel, or at least by a family member. I did meet a Master Teacher . . . but Maggi came first. After all, she had been close "family" for many years, and whoever is responsible for setting up the "Welcome Wagon" over there certainly knew what a delightful experience it would be for me to be greeted by her.

So Maggi and I were interacting on a finer wavelength, and although we had dropped our physical vehicles, our bodies were made visible to the senses through an image in the mind projected as form—and she was as real to see and touch as she was when I'd held her in my arms in the physical world.

My friend Maggi and I walked side by side as we had so many times in that other place of being. Without any effort we moved through a realm of ecstatic color. The pulsating, indescribable colors were fluid—energy waiting to be formed. Maggi showed me how to shape forms out of energy by pressing with my mind. If you want the form to hold, you press firmly. This is a highly mental plane, and form is created with no bodily effort. An image of that which you wish to create is held in mind, and through intense focus is brought into expression. You can lock it in, or release it.

Maggi and I played in the color field, stepping into various hues and feeling their particular vibration. The matchless quality of the colors fascinated me because I hadn't seen anything like them before, and cannot to this day find words to describe the beauty of the shades and hues.[3]

The joy STE-ers express in seeing departed special pets is also indescribable, but sadly, many religious traditions have inferred that humans are at the top of the food chain and are the only living creatures who possess a soul. I believe this is an arrogant assumption. If humans are the only ones who make it through the door to the next level of existence, why do animals keep showing up in STEs? With the next account, a pre-death dream, a whole herd of wonderful pets are seen romping in a celestial afterlife.

I SAW A NEW HEAVEN

As I projected further along, floating on waves with a feeling of something pushing me and holding me at the same time, I passed lots of colors, blues and purples and white and green fields laden with yellow. Jumping and playing in the fields were the animals I had known and loved. I saw Queenie and Princess and Sophie, Sammy and Cindy. I saw C. P. and Ashley and the four guinea pigs. How wonderful to see them again.

This woman also saw her deceased mother, father, siblings, an aunt, an uncle, and grandparents. One of the classic characteristics of a DBV or pre-death experience is that all of the visitors are deceased! Not only did she see relatives who had passed, but a host of pets who had also moved on.

The strong bond between animals and humans is centuries old. As a matter of fact, within tribal cultures, it was believed that animal spirits or guides protect an individual throughout a lifetime. "Guardian spirits almost always appear in animal form. . . . In animal form they can converse with humans. The animal form is rooted in the deep belief that humans and animals are related to one another."[4]

Why is it so difficult for so many in society to believe that as we make our way to the other side, special pets will be there to protect, comfort, and love us as they did in life? Part of the problem involves living in a death-phobic society. Modern science has difficulty seeing that physical death is just a transition from this world to the next. Current ideas regarding the function of the physical body have convinced many of us that once the brain dies, our existence also ends. Because of this, many dying individuals feel frightened as death draws near. Interestingly, a deathbed vision eases the dying process for the departing spirit and reassures us that physical death is not the end.

In the next account, we have another DBV involving a beloved pet. Notice how joyful the ill man becomes.

LUCY IN HEAVEN

My father had been ill and I knew in my heart he would be leaving us very soon. I went to see him that day, and as I walked into his room, I thought for an instant I was in another's room. The man in the bed looked younger than Dad. But it was Dad. He didn't even look up at me as I entered the room. He was looking elsewhere, but he looked like he was seeing something very pleasant. I asked him what he was looking at, and he asked me how I liked the lovely water, trees, and flowers. He was so happy. He said his Lucy was playing near the water with a bunch of other dogs and cats. His Lucy was a bassett hound and Dad had loved this dog with all his heart. He said he could smell the flowers and added that the water ran so pretty and clear in the brook. A few hours later, I lost one of my best friends, my Dad.

Lucy proves modern science wrong, and this father passes peacefully, with a smile on his face.

As we have seen, I have found that animals are present in many STEs. Am I the only one who has seen this? No, there are many others, but there is one researcher I must mention. Biologist and author Rupert Sheldrake, Ph.D., not only studied philosophy at Harvard, but taught at Cambridge. This man of serious science was the director of studies in biochemistry and cell biology at Clare College. Interestingly, in recent years, his research has revolved around the psychic behavior of a variety of animals, ranging from dogs to ferrets. At last count, this English researcher had collected 2,700 case histories of pets exhibiting unexplained psychic behavior.[5] Dr. Sheldrake's book, *Dogs That Know When Their Owners Are Coming Home—And Other Unexplained Powers of Animals*, is full of research supporting the notion that there is much more to our critter friends than fur, scales, and feathers.

The thought of sharing STEs can produce an overwhelming sense of fear. When such encounters involve animals, we can be downright resistant to opening our mouths.

Several STE investigators suggested I not include a chapter on animal encounters in this book. I was told such an addition would discredit the rest of the book, giving the skeptics something more to ridicule. Fifteen years ago I would have followed this advice, but not today. The evidence involving STEs and animals can no longer be ignored.

Earlier, we examined those mystical experiences that had convinced experiencers that we are all one, all connected. The spiritual essence residing within my animals, Broadway, Tom, Mystic, Scrappy, Berry, and Cherry, is vibrant and bright. My essence is not only very much entwined with my pets, but also with all living creatures. I, for one, wouldn't have it any other way. How about you?

chapter seven

Close Encounters of a Family Kind

Call it a clan, call it a network, call it a tribe, call it a family. Whatever you are, whoever you are, you need one.

—Jane Howard, author (1935–1996)

When I released my last book on deathbed visions, I received oodles of e-mail and letters from readers who had questions about family reunions in the world beyond. These concerns ranged from, "Will I see my beloved child, spouse, sibling, parents, or grandparents on the other side when I die?" to "If I have had problems with a particular family member and I still have painful feelings about this, will I have to deal with this person in the afterlife?" With those eager for a reunion, it was a delight to share STE encounters such as this one.

A PARTY IN THE SKY

My favorite aunt passed. . . . Before she left, she spoke of seeing her deceased father, my grandfather, standing at the foot of her bed. She said she saw him as clear as day, and that he said they were all waiting for her to come and they would have a big celebration when she arrived. "They" meaning other friends and relatives in our family who had passed on over the years.

After the funeral for my aunt, her daughter, [who is] my cousin, claimed to have had a vision one night after retiring for the evening. In this vision, she saw her mother, my deceased aunt, waving goodbye to her as she (my aunt) was being greeted by her own father, the deceased father she spoke of visiting her at her deathbed. My aunt appeared as a young woman to my cousin, the way she says she remembered her looking in earlier days. My cousin also said her deceased father, my uncle, was there to greet my aunt, along with several other undistinguishable "beings of light." After waving goodbye, my cousin said my aunt then turned, walked into the light, and disappeared with the others.

With this joyous afterlife family reunion, we have both a DBV and an ADC. As the aunt is getting ready to pass, loving family members, who had already made the trip to the next world, greet her. DBVs ease passage from this life to the next, and this case is no exception.

After the funeral, the daughter receives a wonderful ADC from her mother. During this spiritually dramatic encounter, the daughter sees her mother surrounded by loving relatives who have also passed on. This beautiful reunion eases her grief and loss.

During each of these fantastic meetings, both the deceased and the living exchange greetings across the abyss separating this world from the next. Great joy is experienced, and the fear of death is eradicated. It's just like any other family get-together, only in this situation, the living are receiving loving "hellos" from those in spirit.

Typically, funerals can bring up all sorts of emotion. There is sadness about the passing of the loved one, and there can be uneasiness with death, dying, coffins, cemeteries, and issues surrounding beliefs about life after death.

When was the last time you went to a funeral and felt happy afterwards? The next otherworldly reunion took place during a funeral at a Catholic church. The STE-er who shared this account had a wonderful encounter, which left him not only happy, but feeling very special. His aunt had passed, but physical life was not the end for her.

WE ARE ALL TOGETHER NOW
AND WE'RE HAPPY

About two-thirds of the way through the funeral, while we were standing for prayers, it seemed that I could see my aunt standing in front of me, in sort of a window where there wasn't a window, with my father and my mother on either side of her. My father's mother and stepfather soon joined them, and so did my father's brother, the husband of the aunt who died. All of these people were already dead. My father's brother was wearing a Navy uniform, and I never saw him dressed that way while alive. All six people seemed to be smiling and waving to me, and without actually hearing any words, I got the message: "We're all together now and we're happy. Have fun!" I wanted to point this vision out to my cousin, who was standing next to me, but something told me she wouldn't be able to see it anyway, that it was meant for me.

The above ADC let this man know that those beloved family members who had left this world were reunited as a family on the other side. They were happy and they wanted him to be happy. What a way to end a funeral!

Unfortunately, life's dramas and traumas do not always end with the funeral, and sometimes the thought of contact with certain deceased family members or acquaintances can reopen old wounds. Below is an example of this fear. This following question came from an elderly woman who had had enough ADC experiences and encounters with the unusual to know physical death is not the end. As her own passing neared, fear of death was the least of her worries. What plagued her was concern about meeting up in the afterlife with certain deceased family members who had harmed her in this life.

Fear of Meeting up with Those Who Hurt Us

What about contacts with those who have hurt us so deeply on this side? Since my illness, those friends and family who love me have repeatedly visited me in dreams and visions. However, never have I encountered my father or others who severely hurt me in this life. I have (tried) forgiving them, especially my father, but it is almost impossible. They have never appeared to me or contacted me in dreams. What do I need to anticipate in that regard?

In Spite of Physical Death, Healing Can Happen

Before venturing into premonitions, spiritual awakenings, and the afterlife, I regularly lectured on topics ranging from trauma, abuse, and addiction to healing past hurts, healthy family relationships, and forgiveness.

Over the years, I have worked with thousands of dysfunctional families and have been blessed to be a part of their healing process. Regardless of the loss suffered or the depth of the hurt endured, healing is almost always possible. Even if those who have injured us have passed on, we can still do the work we need to do to heal.

My father was involved in a lot of criminal activity, and let's just say he wasn't a very nice guy. Along with this, he was extremely abusive and highly addicted to a number of mood-altering substances. Sadly, my mother did not protect me or my sisters from his violent lifestyle. My recognition of her lack of protection was more devastating to me than the direct hurt I suffered at the hands of my father. When she died, I thought death would be the barrier that would keep me from making peace with her.

Death did not prevent me from healing. Even though my mother was now living across the steep, wide valley separating this world from the next, I did the work I needed to do to make contact with her. I wrote letters and read them at her grave. While holding pieces of my mother's jewelry, I had heated conversations with her in my mind's eye.

At night, before my head hit the pillow, I would look at photographs of her. Then, I would close my eyes, visualize my mother in my mind's eye, tell her we had unfinished business, and ask her to come visit me in my dreams. The symbolism in my dreams alerted me to where I was in my healing process with my mother. Visitations from her during dreamtime allowed me to do the confrontational work I needed to do to recover from the pain and loss I had suffered during childhood.

There once was a time when I was terrified of the thought of an afterlife reunion with my mother, but not today. By reaching through the veil separating this world from the next, I was able to clear away the wreckage of my past history with my mother and make peace.

Mom and I have done a lot of work since her physical passing, and periodically we have to do a bit more. Her bodily death has not been a deterrent to my healing and I strongly believe our work has helped to heal her, too. When my time comes to depart from the material world, I know my mother will be standing at the edge of the afterlife, waiting to greet me with open arms.

All families have their ups and downs. As George Bernard Shaw said decades ago, "If you cannot get rid of the family skeleton, you may as well make it dance." Working through our family hurts and losses on this side is crucial. Unfortunately, because some hurts run so deep, healing during this lifetime might seem impossible.

The next otherworldly encounter involves a fantastic DBV. During this vision, a woman who has had to live for years with the devastation of an unthinkable loss finally experiences a reunion with loved ones she never thought she'd see again.

A GREEK CELEBRATION IN THE AFTERLIFE

They were both from Greece, both concentration camp survivors. My father lost all but one brother, a couple of cousins, and one aunt. My mother lost her entire family in Auschwitz. They met after liberation, fell in love, and married. After my oldest brother and I were born in Greece, they immigrated to the United States. Here, we grew up, along with two younger brothers and a sister.

Two and a half years ago, my father died following a heart attack and stroke that left his brain completely destroyed, with no chance of recovery. . . . One night, after being bedridden by illness for three weeks, he sat up in bed, reached his arms into the air, and then lay back dead. As he reached up, my mother had said, "Go to your mamika, darling." *Mamika* is a Greek term of endearment for mother.

After my father's passing, my mother's grief was so deep. My father was the first person she had loved after losing so many loved ones in the Birkenau and Auschwitz concentration camps. She just wanted to die; it was an impossible situation, as her heartbreak over my father's death was so intense. With heartbreak came stomach pains. After many tests . . . they opened her up . . . and then immediately closed her up. [Because of the extent of her cancer] there was nothing to do but send her home to die.

. . . I had been living in New York . . . in a very lucrative career in the entertainment industry. The minute the doctors said it was over, I quit my job, sold my co-op . . . returned [home], and spent the rest of my mother's life with her. . . .

We (my family and I) were on deathwatch. One morning, she kept saying something in Greek. None of us speak Greek, so I called Betty, a friend whose aunt had been Linda, my mother's friend who had died in Auschwitz. Betty translated the word as best as she could as a kind of storm, but not a weather storm, more like a happening, a big celebration, and a storm of people. Betty then offered to come over so she could help to take care of all the family, cook, and be there if my mother started speaking Greek again. Her own parents and sister had passed away, as had her twenty-six-year-old daughter, and my mother had been a sort of surrogate mother to her. . . .

So, Betty came over and started cooking. Later on, my mother started calling her by her Greek name, Bondi. She rushed into my mother's room asking, "What is it, Solica?" My mother was speaking to her in Greek, and as she responded to Mother in Greek she also translated for us what was being said. "Your mother is here cooking," my mother said to her, and she replied, "No, I'm here cooking." My mother then said,

"Bondi, I know you are here cooking for my children and grandchildren, but your mother and [aunt] are cooking, too, for the celebration." Her mother is deceased and the aunt is my mother's best friend, who died in Auschwitz. My mother then added, "Diane [the twenty-six-year-old daughter who had recently passed] is also here." With this, Betty began to sob.

Then my mother began greeting others in her family (all deceased), telling them where they were going to sit. Her eyes were closed and her hand moved around the bedspread. "Henriette [the name of a deceased sister] will sit here, Mamika [her mother] here, and where's Bella [the name of another sister who had died in the camp]? Has anyone seen her?" She continued to seat my father and everyone in her family, except for her adored older sister, Bella, who wasn't there. When the youngest brother (also deceased) joined the group, she put her hand up in the air and in a delighted voice said, "Oh, Leoniki [name of this brother], hi!" This continued for nearly an hour, and it's mostly on tape, as I turned on the tape recorder, but it's in Greek!

We were all awed, amazed, and comforted. We were all crying at how beautiful this was. And, there were ten of us in the room who witnessed this.

. . . In the middle of the night, she started speaking to someone in Spanish. As we are Sephardic Jews, both Spanish and Greek was spoken in my mother's girlhood home. She kept saying Bella. My older brother Jerry and his wife were in the guest room. . . . He speaks Spanish fluently. He asked my mother to whom she was talking, and she said, "Bella." He asked her where she was, and she said "B—'s house." He then asked her what they were discussing, and she said, "B— wants me to go for a walk with her." "What are you telling her, Mom?" he asked. She replied, "That I'm not ready to go for a walk yet." She talked a bit more to Bella, and that was all they discussed, going for a walk.

Two days later, my mother passed in the night, as she softly called out to her sister Bella. I feel confident that her adored older sister came to get her to take her to the celebration, as they had all (those on the other side) missed her so much.

The gift of my mother's visions has had a powerful influence on my life. Although I was raised Jewish, I didn't know a lot about it. So, I decided to go on a spiritual journey . . . to learn more about the mystical side of Judaism, and have found a sense of peace. . . . I am not afraid to die, as I know my parents and friends who have gone before me will come back to get me.

My priorities in life are completely different. I spent years in the entertainment industry, and although it was a very good time, I never had the serenity I have now . . . all the stress that friends have seen on my face is gone. I don't know yet what I want to do with the second act of my life, but I do know it includes public service . . . I spend all the time I can volunteering for various organizations. I deliver Meals on Wheels to the elderly and homebound twice a week, volunteer in a hospital emergency room three times a week, and help out once in a while with other organizations and special events, such as fund raising.

Not long ago, I received an e-mail from Dorothy. She shared with me that her niece and nephew had recently celebrated their bat mitzvah and bar mitzvah. The whole family had come together for this joyous occasion. She also added that the family had strongly sensed the presence of her beloved parents. Death cannot separate the love that bonds a family together.

Spiritually transformative experiences can also give us bits

and pieces of information about our difficult family relationships. During a trip to Scotland and England, I was researching
a mystical order called the Knights Templar. Formed in Europe
around 1099, during the Crusades, the Knights Templar assisted
religious pilgrims in safe travel to Jerusalem. Because of persecution, the knights eventually moved their order underground
and many scattered to the English countryside and Scottish
Highlands.[1]

In London, there remains one of the few Knights Templar
churches.[2] This church in particular, circular in shape and con-
secrated in 1185, had grabbed my curiosity and I was anxious to
have a good look at it. Upon arrival, I immediately felt very
emotional and anxious, so much so that I asked Michael to take
the boys for a walk outside the church. I have always felt
extremely connected to the history of the United Kingdom, but
as I stood in the church, taking in the drama of centuries past,
I knew something "different" was about to happen.

Tears began streaming down my face, and I felt as though I
had been there before. It was overwhelming, and I finally had
to sit down. Out of the blue came a brief vision of myself as my
father's caretaker. Interestingly, the time period for this experience was not current. The revelation took my breath away.

During childhood, living with my father was a nightmare.
For years, I could not understand why he was so full of hate.
Time eventually revealed life conditions, which explained some
of his angry behavior. In spite of this, I still felt in the depth of
my soul that there was more to it than this. Sitting in this lovely
historic building, enlightenment hit me like a ton of bricks. My
history with my father had not begun with this lifetime. Our
history went back several lifetimes.

Eventually, I was able to piece together one of these past
lifetimes, and this allowed me to understand that my father's

current anger was not for me to resolve. This was his mission, and there was nothing I could do about it. With such awareness, I no longer felt it was my responsibility to make my relationship with my father work. It was his journey, and I was powerless over the road he chose to travel. This profound STE allowed me to forgive my father and also enabled me to love the spiritual essence that resides within him.

Our family connections are strong, regardless of the circumstances involved. Unfinished business can be finished, and healing can take place. My book *Learning to Say No* addresses the healing of both current and past family-related wounds.[3]

When a passing occurs, many of us are left feeling guilty over things not said or action not taken. Sometimes we are very helpless over these situations. Circumstances can prevent us not only from following through on promises made, but from being at a departing loved one's side. The hurt and guilt resulting from this can be lifelong. Thankfully, our "sixth sense" can be our remedy. Such was the case for the mother of the woman who related the following ADC example.

After being in a coma for four days, a dying man in England called for his family to gather around him. He wanted to say goodbye and to share a vision with them. A granddaughter related the experience.

A LOVING CONNECTION BETWEEN A FATHER, A MOTHER, AND A DAUGHTER

My grandmother asked him what he had been staring at and he replied, "You don't see her?" My grandmother asked, "Who?" and he replied, "I have been watching my mother [deceased]. She has come to take me home." He died that afternoon and, unfortunately, my mom was unable to attend his funeral because she had to fly back home to the United States.

For the next thirty years, my mom had a recurring dream about a wonderful garden with many roses and other flowers. The one thing that always stuck out in her dream was an archway of climbing roses.

In 1990, my mother visited her sister in England, and the two of them went to my grandfather's grave. The memorial garden he was buried in had all of the exact features in her dream, including the arch with the climbing roses.

Even though this woman was unable to attend her father's funeral, she was blessed with a vision of her own. Her nightly dreams provided her with a snapshot view of just where her father's remains were. Dreams can provide us with a doorway to the next level of existence. Visitation to once-imagined, invisible realms can reunite us with loved ones we never thought we would see again. Such reunions can also provide us with premonitions of things to come. This was the case with the next spiritual adventure. With the following near-death experience, a husband and wife began their joint STE by having the same dream.

GRANDMA IS WATCHING OVER THE LITTLE ONE

One night I was dreaming that I was dying, and next to me in bed, my husband was also dreaming that I was dying. Bothered by the dream, my husband forced himself to wake up. He then reached for me and noticed I was stone cold. With this, he lifted my arms and they fell limp.

By this time, I realized I was outside of my body, standing in the mouth of a tunnel, watching my husband jump up, scream, and try to lift me. I then turned and entered the tunnel. . . . My husband was still screaming and shaking me wildly. I felt bad, but I had to go into the tunnel. . . . (She then encounters a bright light and has a brief conversation about her entry into the tunnel) . . . we talked and I asked if I could come in. He gave me a choice, and as we continued discussing this choice, I could hear my son and my great-grandmothers' voices. . . . I got a glimpse of my son and I asked, "Is that my son?" He [the brilliant light] told me yes and then added that my grandmother was looking after him. Interestingly, my son had been a three-week-old baby when he died, and he now looked to be two years of age. I said [to the brilliant light], "I didn't know you can grow in heaven." After talking awhile [the brilliant light] told me that my husband was going to be in need of me and that this experience was as much for him as it was for me. [The light] also told me of a daughter that was to be born to me, and he also shared a few things about her [nine years later she was born].

I had no choice but to return, so I made the journey back through the tunnel, stopped, and looked at my husband. He was crying and getting ready to call for help on the telephone, but then started to shake me again. I then stepped out of the tunnel . . . [and was back in the body].

My husband told me of his dream, and before he could finish, I told him what I saw him doing and of my experience. . . . Due to fear that those around us would not see us as solid people, it was at least ten years later before we ever told anyone of our experience. . . . My husband said I had no pulse, I wasn't breathing, and that he had worked on me for two hours.

Here we have a fascinating account, but the experiencers are fearful of sharing this experience with friends and loved ones. This is such a sad commentary on how society receives encounters of this nature. A reunion between a deceased child, beloved deceased grandmother, and the experiencer provides reassurance that life continues after physical death. A glimpse into the future is also offered to the couple. After wondering whether or not she will ever be blessed with the birth of another child, this experiencer is told to expect a daughter. But, does she feel safe telling others about this? Sadly, the answer is no.

Wouldn't it be wonderful if we could openly share all of our STE encounters with those we love? I believe it would be, but fear of ridicule often forces us to lock away our precious experiences. Finding people to discuss such things with can be difficult at best. If we do take a risk and begin talking about our STEs, we can find ourselves in a predicament. In the next account, a dying man had an interesting reunion with several deceased family members. Unfortunately, the priest who was sent to care for him was unable to be supportive of this man's wonderful reunion.

THE UNAWARE PRIEST

An elderly man was preparing to pass in a nursing home. His mind was quite sharp and he was very aware of current events. The nurses caring for him said he was a "gentle soul" and very spiritual. One morning, a care worker entered his room to find him wide awake. When she asked him if he had slept well, he replied that no, he hadn't. She then asked why and he said he wasn't able to sleep because of all of the people who were in his room. When the nurse then asked what people, he replied that his mother and father had visited him (both deceased, as the gentleman was in his late nineties) along with a number of other people. He then asked her if she saw the woman standing in the corner. Looking toward the corner of the room, she saw no one.

She then asked him if he wanted to speak to a priest. He said yes, and she sent for one. The priest and the elderly gentleman talked together for about an hour. As the priest was leaving, the nurse shared the older man's visions. After hearing this, he told the nurse, "It was only stress." This answer did not satisfy the nurse because she did not believe the elderly gentleman was suffering from any stress at all. If anything, he seemed incredibly calm, relaxed, and happy. Four weeks later, the man passed. It appears as though this clergy person was reluctant to consider that just maybe this elderly man was having a reunion with loving deceased relatives.

Thankfully, an aware healthcare giver was able to validate this man's experience. Wouldn't it be just incredible if more clergy people were able to be more open to such encounters? As a rabbi friend of mine once said, "Clergy, who are supposed to be supportive of spiritual happenings, are often more skeptical than hard-core scientists!"

On many occasions, caring nurses at the bedside of the dying are the only ones who are able to support STE reunions. Over the years, society has bred an atmosphere of mistrust in otherworldly affairs, and this belief has trickled down into the basic family unit. Not only do many family members have difficulty talking about topics involving dying, spirituality, life after death, the sixth sense, or "things that go bump in the night," but many times they don't know how to "be there" and "listen" to those who have encountered such happenings.

Because of this, I continue to brim over with gratitude for loving, helpful professionals who are able to assist and support

STE-ers. In the following example, the patient's family was unavailable, but a nurturing nurse pushed aside her own fear and was there to offer support.

HE WAS NOT AFRAID, BUT AT FIRST, I WAS

I am an RN who has taken care of many elderly people. One night . . . I cared for a man who I am sure spent the whole night seeing and talking to deceased relatives. He then passed away the next morning. He was not afraid, but at first, I was, in the lone of the night, feeling like I didn't belong there in his special time of commune and crossing over.

I was working private-duty shift with him while he was in a nursing home, and during the night shift none of his family was present. If he had spent his last hours with his family, they would have seen what I saw, and it might have been significant to them. He spoke to the "people" by name, and one was his mother. I felt out of place and regret that he spent his time with me, a total stranger working at her job, instead of his loved ones.

This man was very lucky to have this nurse at his side. Sadly, even if family is there, they often times are still at a loss as to how to talk about STEs. Most parents don't talk to their children about such matters, so how can we expect youngsters to grow into adults capable of discussing otherworldly encounters?

Interestingly, over the years, I have developed a bit of a reputation in my neighborhood as the woman who "understands these things." On several occasions, parents have come to me to share concern about an ADC one of their children has had.

Recently, I hosted a small dinner party and invited several

neighbors from down the street. The adults sat in one room, caught up with one another and enjoying the meal, while the children ran up and down the stairs, playing hide and seek. When I let everyone know that dessert was about to be served, the children scrambled downstairs to join the adults. I asked the children to help me clear away all the tableware. Looking forward to a thick slice of chocolate brownie topped with fudge frosting, I received no argument.

While rinsing and loading dishes into the dishwasher, one of my young guests said, "I heard you talking at dinner about the photographs your other neighbor had taken of the spirit." Living in an area of the city that was built in the late 1880s, spiritual activity is often reported by the residents. Galveston Island was devastated by a powerful hurricane in 1900. This natural catastrophe left 9,000 people dead, with bodies stacked in the streets where my neighbors and I currently live. Tales of the 1900 storm had been shared during mealtime, and it was obvious to me that the young man stacking dishes had gotten an earful.

While my arms were elbow-deep in soapsuds, the young man went on to describe how he had seen the spirit of an old man in his house. He added that a pungent smell accompanied the sighting. I asked him if the spirit visitation frightened him, and he responded, "Well, sort of, but what really freaked me out was that awful smell."

As I served dessert, I asked the youngster's father about the sighting and he validated it. He added that he had also seen strange blue orbs floating around the house and that his wife had reported that the electrical appliances were acting strangely. She was also aware of the nasty smell that coincided with the old man's spiritual visitation and had tried to neutralize it with strong incense.

After sharing information with them about the various forms of spirit manifestation I had encountered, the family began sharing with one another more openly. Today, the family continues to investigate the history of their house, along with the surrounding property, in order to determine what might be behind the excessive spiritual activity they had all experienced.

Talking about STEs can feel downright impossible! As one family member said to me, "Where do you begin? We never talked about such things before. Won't people think we are nuts?"

This next wonderful account is one of my favorites. After the STE occurred, this family never discussed it. I truly believe they didn't know how.

For this man, his upcoming passing was no excuse for poor manners, even if the visitors were not visible to others at the bedside.

WELL, WHY DON'T YOU SERVE THEM SOME REFRESHMENTS?

At the time, I didn't understand just what it was my grandfather was talking about; neither did my mother or my aunt, who were also present. Everyone thought he (my grandfather) was just having hallucinations.

As we were all there by his bedside, he turned and looked at us and said, "Well, why don't you serve some refreshments? Can't you see that my wife, three children, and mother are all here visiting me?"

We didn't know what to make of this remark, but now I understand. My mother has since passed, and we never discussed this experience while she was alive.

Acceptance of STEs begins in the home. If we raise our children to be open to other spiritual realms, they will grow into adults who feel confident in talking about such occurrences. In the years to come, they will then pass this tradition on to their own children. Fear of death will not be an issue, and the gift of the living experience will take on more purpose and meaning. Being aware that there is more to existence than meets the eye actually sets the stage for encountering wonderful spiritual adventures. Here is a wonderful example of just how a parent's acceptance of STEs can trickle down to the following generation. Openly discussing communication between this reality and the next can positively impact all involved.

THE STE—A FAMILY TRADITION

I grew up listening to my mom talk of goings-on and personally was visited by my dad in dreams regularly after he passed when I was ten. I have had so many lucid dreams of loved ones who have passed that I interview and question them and try to take notes in my dream. I have a detailed journal by my bed. Before my brother passed from cancer in 1998, I told him to come to me in my dreams, and he has done a great job. He has also given us very striking "coincidences," which amaze people. I could relate to just about everything you spoke of, including the very strict religious relative who thinks I'm dealing with Satan.

A little over a week ago, my nephew Nick, age thirty, was killed instantly in a car accident. He is the son of my deceased brother. My daughter, age fifteen, was having a really tough time since he was like a brother to her, and last week we were really concerned about her and the depression she was experiencing. She couldn't make it through school after the funeral, was not caring about her commitment to the golf team she is on, was watching videos of him, pouring through photo albums for his pictures, and telling us she hated her life, was depressed, and didn't care. She woke last Friday to tell me of her dream. A young man was walking toward her and she wished he were Nickie, since so many of his friends resemble him. As he approached, she saw it *was* Nickie, and his eyes were so blue. He didn't say anything but starting hugging her very tightly. She said he was *so strong*, but not muscle strong, even though he had worked out every day. He was generating so much energy that it was pushing her back. She woke and was more focused than she had been since we received the news. He could see how she was suffering and needed help the most in our family. She has already written about her dream in a journal and is proud of how the family was uplifted by it. He truly has given my daughter one last hug, but it has extended to all of us.

Perhaps a perfect reality involves more than the house we live in, the job we go to, the food we eat, and the neighborhood surrounding us. I believe if we allowed ourselves to be aware of just how often the invisible world is intertwined with the everyday living experience, there would be more tolerance for our neighbor, increased care for the environment, a stronger desire to resolve conflict and hurt, a change in our priorities, less war, poverty, and violence, and more commitment to personal responsibility in every area of our lives. Does this sound like utopia? How about heaven on earth?

chapter eight

STEs Providing Love and Assistance During Tragic Times

The good, the bad, hardship, joy, tragedy, love,
and happiness are all interwoven into one
indescribable whole that one calls life. You
cannot separate the good from the bad, and
perhaps there is no need to do so.

—Jacqueline Bouvier Kennedy Onassis, former First Lady (1929–1994)

*W*ithin many religious traditions, it is understood that no matter how devastating the tragedy or painful the loss, there is always a silver lining. Goodness rises from the ashes of the phoenix, and such blessings might come in many forms. My mother's early death is responsible for my current professional endeavors, which involve assisting those who are in grief. My husband's exposure to relatives who had suffered the terror of the Holocaust as children cast in stone his desire to work with youngsters.

When a person of the Jewish faith dies, the family says a specific prayer every week for a year. This ancient Aramaic prayer is called the Kaddish. The words of this beautiful verse praise God with promises of song and adorations. After glorifying creation, the prayer ends with, "May the One who causes peace to reign in high heavens, let peace descend on us . . . "[1]

In saying this prayer, those mourning loss reaffirm their faith in a "Greater Good." Even while in the throes of distress, the mourner acknowledges that in spite of grief, creation is still a gift, life continues, and that tragedy is a part of life. In this way, tragedy and the beauty of life are forever linked. Personally and professionally, I have also found this to be true.

Most of my own STEs have involved tragedy of one sort or another. My first out-of-body experience was the byproduct of violent sexual betrayal. This OBE allowed me to survive a terrible time in my life. Years later, I recalled this trauma when a vision abruptly visited me. In the vision, I re-experienced this dreadful day by looking down upon myself, as I floated above my fragile young body.

SURVIVING BETRAYAL WITH AN STE

It's afternoon naptime, but my father has come into the room. His voice is booming. He is wearing dark slacks and a V-neck T-shirt. His dark hair is swept back, and I can see the rage in his eyes. The little girl is being pulled out of her bed. Her grandmother recently permed her blond hair, and she now has a head full of curls. The little girl can't be more than four or five years old. Wearing only a lime green sun suit, she seems incredibly vulnerable.

I'm watching them from above and can see everything crystal clear. It's very frightening and I feel sick to my stomach as I stare at the scene below, but I can do nothing to protect her.

My father is extremely angry. He grabs the little girl and violently assaults her, both physically and sexually. It's just terrible, and I know she is having a difficult time breathing. I can see the scene fully and completely. At first, I'm just overwhelmed with what I'm seeing. I had no idea he had been so violent with me. Then the real pain creeps in; and as I realize the little girl was me, I'm in agony over the betrayal.

Thank goodness I had an OBE! Dissociating from my body, leaving my physical self while my father hurt me, enabled me not to have to feel, emotionally, physically, or spiritually, the incredible shame, pain, and terror he was inflicting upon me. After the offense, the OBE then allowed me to tuck this trauma into the dark recesses of my subconscious. Only in this way was I able to sit down to dinner calmly with my father and the rest of my family that night.

As a young child, I didn't have the emotional maturity to know how to heal from this trauma, nor did I have healthy caretakers to turn to for comfort. My OBE sheltered me. Up until adulthood, my out-of-body experience kept me somewhat safe and allowed me to function, and I believe it actually kept me alive. Years later, in adulthood, I was better prepared to handle the truth about this tragedy. Once I had taken the time to feel the feelings about my past and embrace the reality of my trauma, I was then able to have true appreciation for the STE that had protected me.

Am I alone with regard to my particular STE encounter? No, sadly I'm not. Years ago, I recognized that many sexual abuse survivors have had OBEs during incidents of violence. As a clinician, what I have found is that the majority of STE encounters occur shortly after a tragedy, death, or life trauma. Witnesses to murder, war, and other types of devastation or violence have also survived because of an OBE. In my therapy practice as a specialist in trauma, I have worked with thousands of sexual assault survivors and numerous trauma victims who found it necessary to flee the physical body when the emotional, physical, sexual, or spiritual suffering began. Because of this, I have discussed this amazing survival skill in several of my books.

Spiritually, I believe little children are protected from the tragedies in life in numerous ways, especially when there are no caretakers available to take up the task. Adults swirling within the vortex of life devastation and tragedy can also be protected with an STE. An out-of-body experience is just one of those amazing survival skills.

When working with trauma survivors who have had such spiritual encounters, I find it is essential to discuss them. Too many healthcare professionals dismiss not only STEs, but also those associated with trauma. Some of my peers even refer to experiences of this nature as a type of mental illness. This just isn't so, but in spite of this, the prescription pad often comes out and a strong anti-psychotic medication is given to the traumatized or grieving individual who attempts to discuss STEs openly.

STEs can be used to assist in the healing process. Instead of medicating them away, they need to be appreciated and explored. Read the following account to see what I mean.

A TRUE GUARDIAN ANGEL

I see myself looking down on myself. I'm on the ceiling. Oh my God. My uncle has taken all of my clothes off and he is doing unspeakable things to me. The little girl below, the little girl who is me, is numb, totally rigid. It's like she is dead. She's like a rag doll.

It's all too much, so I leave. I find myself floating away. I've got to get away, so I fly through the ceiling, up to the sky, toward the universe. The stars are just incredible. I feel so free, but I don't stop. Suddenly, I'm in a room, a beautiful room. It's so safe in here. The room is pink and its full of stuffed animals. I feel so safe.

Then I see her. She is brilliant, absolutely beautiful and brilliant. Golden. I go to her, and she cautiously embraces me. I've been here before. She just hugs me and I sob, sob for the little girl down there, sob for what he is doing to her. We then sit in a big chair and she takes me into her lap, holds me, strokes my hair, and tells me it's okay. I ask her if I have come here before, and she says, "Yes, I am always here for you."

The floor of the room has an opening in it and we look at the little girl being molested by my uncle. I ask this angel, "How will she survive?" The angel says, "I will help her."

I worked with this woman for several years. As a patient, she was reluctant to discuss anything of a spiritual nature. Interestingly, she was a lay pastor at her church and initially had come to see me because she was having difficulty believing in God. She said she felt like a phony when called upon by her congregation to discuss spiritual matters. As we explored her childhood history, she unveiled numerous acts of violence committed against her by family members.

Since our first concept of God is derived from the characteristics of those who take care of us during childhood, is it any wonder this woman was having problems with believing in some sort of loving Higher Power? Her childhood "higher powers" had hurt and abused her. After we sorted out her trauma and redefined her understanding of a loving universal life force, she was ready to take a real look at the guardian angel who had protected her from feeling her physical and sexual abuse during childhood. Her STE provided a new spiritual beginning, one that was more authentic for her. This is often the case when an STE is encountered during tragedy.

Spiritual experiences associated with tragedy can ease healing and open a door to future spiritual growth. The following story is very overwhelming and frightening, but the woman in this account discovered that adversity can be conquered and that nothing in life is impossible.

DYING KEPT ME ALIVE

At the age of seven I was raped and nearly murdered by a stranger who broke his way into my grandmother's house. I happened to be home alone. . . . One of the odd things that I remembered from the event was the fact that I was being smothered and I knew I was dying. I then left my body and was actually watching what this man was doing to me from a completely different vantage point. . . . I was sitting on the floor next to the bed. And I could see this man on top of me. . . .

I've suffered from depression all of my life (or at least since I've been seven years old). I've been to numerous physicians and therapists. I've tried [a number of medications] and psychotherapy. But the nightmares never went away. That is, until last year, when I met a man who taught me how to meditate. And the nightmares stopped immediately. Since that time, I've only had a couple of recurrences. . . . I continue to meditate twice a day for twenty-minute sessions, in the morning and in the evening. . . . Transcendental meditation really does work for PTSD (post-traumatic stress disorder).

Transcendental meditation, used appropriately, in conjunction with a recovery program, can assist in healing PTSD. This woman took steps to resolve her trauma using traditional medicine, but found it wasn't enough. Meditation allowed her to do the work necessary to really begin healing from her childhood violation. In my practice, I have noted that individuals who have had STEs during a trauma are more willing to investigate alternative methods of healing, such as support groups, meditation, dance, art therapy, massage, herbal remedies, nutritional support, or unorthodox psychotherapies. Such seekers eventually develop a spiritual way of thinking that incorporates the STE they originally experienced during tragedy.

The Price We Can Pay for Ignoring STEs

A very good friend of mine, British psychic Chris Robinson, had predicted the World Trade Center attacks on September 11, 2001.

A number of years before this tragic national devastation, Chris came to me and asked if I knew of anyone who would be interested in investigating his ability to predict future tragedies. Knowing of Chris's work with Scotland Yard in the United Kingdom, I agreed that it was time for researchers in the States to meet him. I then directed him to Dr. Gary Schwartz, professor of psychology, medicine, neurology, psychiatry, and surgery and director of Human Energy Systems Laboratory at the University of Arizona.

Measuring Precognition Scientifically

Dr. Schwartz has conducted a number of scientific studies on well-known "Hollywood" mediums, such as Sylvia Brown, John

Edward, and James Van Praagh. Much of his well-respected research is dedicated to exploring afterlife communication and other areas related to altered states of consciousness scientifically.

Recently, while researching Chris's capability, Dr. Schwartz scientifically validated my friend's remarkable gift for predicting future events. His article, "Controlled Experiment of Precognitive Dream Intelligence in a Highly Skilled Subject," published in *The Journal for Psychical Research*, discusses these results in detail.

While documenting this research, Chris and Dr. Schwartz spent several weeks together. During that time, my friend had another amazing prediction—one that sadly came true. Dr. Schwartz had this to say about Chris's precognitive dream about the World Trade Center tragedy.

Some Nightmares Do Come True

It is worth noting that while C. R. (Chris Robinson) was in Tucson, he had a "nightmare" involving planes crashing into large buildings in New York City and thousands of people dying. These dreams continued when he returned to England. He recorded these dreams, drew the buildings, and told his police superiors of the dreams. A few days before 9-11, he was compelled to post a letter to the London Embassy warning of a serious threat to U.S. safety.[2]

Wouldn't it be a blessing if society heeded warnings from well-researched or documented individuals who regularly had dreams and premonitions predicting future tragic events? Individuals such as my friend Chris are not the only ones to experience this sort of STE. Many everyday people periodically encounter premonitions about calamities yet to come.

According to journalist Rosemary Ellen Guiley, an author who is also well known for her publications discussing the paranormal, STEs and tragedy seem to go hand in hand. In addressing precognition and the prediction of future events, she had this to say.

> ✿ Precognition is the most frequently reported of all extrasensory perception (ESP) experiences, occurring most often (60 to 70 percent) in dreams. It also happens spontaneously in waking visions, hallucinations, thoughts that flash the mind, and a sense of "knowing" . . . .
>
> The majority of spontaneous precognitive experiences happen within forty-eight hours of the future events, particularly within twenty-four hours. A rare few happen months or even years before actual events take place. Severe emotional shock seems to be a major factor in precognition. By a four-to-one ratio, most concern unhappy events, such as death and dying, illness, accidents, and natural disasters.[3]

Some deathbed visions fall into the category of tragic STEs. Though the passing of a loved one can produce intense sadness, with support from surrounding loved ones, healthy grieving can happen, and as time moves on, healing can begin. As we have seen, the typical DBV involves visions of deceased relatives and friends coming to escort dying loved ones to an afterlife existence. Those left behind have sadness about the afterlife move their loved one has made, but the DBV experience assures them that physical death is not the end. Though this is the usual DBV, it is also important to discuss those encounters, which are the byproduct of sudden tragedy. In the next STE example, we have a perfect example of precognition.

Unfortunately, this little girl had no one to discuss her frightening DBV with.

MY FATHER'S MURDER AND MY EMPATHETIC EXPERIENCE

When I was ten years old, my father was murdered. My father was a bad seed, but I think he had been trying to change. Three nights before my father's death, I dreamt of him dying. Strange dream, but in my house you didn't discuss these things.

On the night of his murder, my sisters and I were sleeping. My older sister woke up to yell at my younger sister and me for talking. We were both asleep, and we were describing in our sleep my father's murder. It was as if we were seeing it through his eyes.

Today, some thirty years later, what has stayed with me most from that dream are the spoke tire rims of a car driving away. Years later, I learned my father was beaten, thrown out of a car, and then shot.

Since that time, I have always seen, dreamt, and felt things. . . . we are all part of the web of life. Time is a man-made thing. There is no beginning or end.

As tragic as this life-altering event was for this woman, a belief in the spiritual interconnection between all of creation is strong. This seeker also adds, "I have always seen, dreamt, and felt things." Individuals who regularly "sense" otherworldly existences, presences, or future events, are often referred to as being a "Sensitive" or an "Intuitive." Sensitives and Intuitives are able to tap into other realities of existence with relative ease.

I believe all of us have the ability to "tune in" to the invisible, but sadly, many of us ignore this hidden part of ourselves. STEs associated with profound tragic events can forcefully push open once-locked doors, allowing for future investigation into this once-closeted sixth sense.

After several traumatic STE encounters, the woman in the following account learned a valuable lesson with regard to trusting her own glimpses of the unusual. Along with this she discovered that these experiences are not unique to her, but are actually very common. Unhappily, she also recognized that few people are willing to talk openly about such encounters.

SPIRITUAL LESSONS LEARNED

I was living overseas in England. . . . I was asleep one night in my dormitory room alone, and I woke in the middle of the night to see a robed figure at the edge of my bed. He had on a worn cloak covering the body and a sack of some sort of the same material over his head, which was tied at the neck with a noose, as though he had been hung. The figure would not move. I blinked again and again and it was still there. I closed my eyes and waited until dawn, then opened them again and it was gone. But I had this horrible feeling of dread for the next few months.

Then my mother called me one night and told me my grandfather had died. He hadn't been ill, but his heart wasn't good, so I assumed that it was heart failure.

When I returned home, about six months later, I eventually found out the truth about my grandfather's death. My mom admitted to me that he had hung himself. . . . too much has happened to me to believe these events are coincidences . . .

The second event also happened when I was overseas. . . . I was heavily involved with a particular young man when I lived overseas. We were very close. It was New Year's and he spent it in London with friends while I stayed at the dorm. Where I lived was about three hours from London.

I went out with friends, but we were home way before midnight. They left and I was alone in my dorm room. At midnight, I heard some commotion outside, but didn't really think anything of it. Then, at about a quarter after midnight, I started pacing around the room, feeling very anxious.

As if someone else were controlling me, I called a cab and had the driver take me to the hospital. There were all sorts of people there, it being New Year's and all. I sat waiting to see a triage nurse for a couple of hours. And, while I sat there, I just stared at the television and the people, and this one guy who was really bloodied up from what looked like a fight. A feeling of panic and terror overwhelmed me. It was horrible.

By the time the nurse saw me, they found nothing wrong and said I was having an anxiety attack. I called a cab and then waited some more. Once I was finally home, I felt panicky, but was tired. So I went to bed and eventually fell asleep.

I didn't hear from my boyfriend for two days. Then he came over and was very upset. He had been with his friends on New Year's Eve, at one guy's flat. Just after midnight, one of these young men came into the room, said, "Happy New Year's" and then shot himself in the head. My boyfriend was the one who went to the hospital with him, where he sat by his side for hours, talking to the guy, though he was, obviously, seriously wounded, until the guy finally died sometime the next morning.

I believe I, too, went to the hospital, because I somehow sensed what was happening with my boyfriend, miles away . . . I was raised in a family who is very accepting of these sorts of experiences, but I still get frustrated. These types of encounters have continued throughout my life, but I have not, as yet, received a satisfactory answer as to "why." These things seem to be very common, yet no one wants to talk about them.

The key words responsible for this woman's ability to readily embrace her experiences are found in the phrase, "I was raised in a family who is very accepting of these sorts of experiences." In spite of this, modern-day society's lack of acceptance continues to create "frustration" for her. Forces not easily visible to the naked eye are touching everyday people every minute of every day. But, unlike generations before us, we as a society seem to be unwilling to "see" what is right before us. Those few of us who do readily, or even cautiously, reach out to make contact with otherworldly presences receive reprimand and ridicule. Accepting that a picture painted with just our five basic senses is incomplete is a frightening prospect for many. Fear of the unknown is society's biggest enemy. For this reason, and this reason alone, discussing STEs openly is basically taboo in our culture.

Regardless of this, when an STE brings comfort and healing, it is difficult to keep tightlipped, no matter who is doing the ridiculing. As I shared earlier, while discussing deathbed visions on the Howard Stern radio show, the radio host and his sidekick, Robin, mocked me terribly. I had agreed to do his show because I knew there were those in his listening audience who needed to hear what I had to say. After the radio program aired, I received tons of e-mail from individuals looking for validation of their own STE encounters. This is one of those letters and, I must add, as tragic as it initially appears, its message of hope and spiritual healing is one of my favorites.

CAN THIS BE TRUE, OR WAS I HALLUCINATING?

Just this year, my younger brother passed on. He was just thirty-one. He and I had always been close (I have two older brothers). The night of his death, before I knew he had passed, I had a dream. . . . I dreamt of my brother. In the dream, he was radiant. He was lit up from within, and he looked so healthy. Just to look at him brought peace to my entire being. He was smiling, and it was beautiful.

Before his death, my brother had gained forty-five pounds, was addicted to various prescription drugs, and was suffering from drug-induced Parkinson's disease, which was the result of his previous heroin addiction.

In the dream, he came to me with a smile on his face that filled me will calmness. I told him, "You look great!" He then laid a hand on my shoulder. I've never felt anything like this before. When he touched me, it was as if my entire being was filled with joy. It was a happiness and sense of tranquility I had never had the pleasure of knowing before. I was then lit up from within with jubilation and radiance.

He told me, "Don't worry," and then said I, too, would "lose the weight." I had gained forty pounds with two pregnancies and was having difficulty getting rid of not only the weight, but also a depression.

After this, he turned and left. During our entire meeting, he and I were surrounded by white light. There was nothing above or below or around us, just white light. He left me in my dream, I don't recall dreaming anymore, and then it was morning.

The next day, they found him in a hotel room (he was on a business trip). . . . He had many pills scattered about. I don't believe he took his own life, but I do believe he overdosed by accident.

As he predicted, I lost all the weight and, except for my grief over my brother's untimely death, most of my sadness. Can this be true, or was I hallucinating like Howard said?

This woman's brother died an addict's death. For those who survive such a loss, the grief can be inconsolable. I know, because I have worked with many, many families who have lost a loved one to drug or alcohol dependency. The disease of chemical addiction to illegal or prescription drugs, or to alcohol, directly impacts one out of every three families in this country.

The DBV experience she had before she even had knowledge of her brother's fatal overdose is a very common one. When DBV experiencers see deceased loved ones during an STE, typically they look younger, healthier, and full of joy. Their only concern at that moment is to comfort the living. Not only does her brother offer her support and love, he also provides her with a prediction about future events to come.

This tragic passing provided several gifts for this woman, but once again, we see society rebuking her experience. It was my pleasure to validate this woman's incredible visitation from her brother.

With the next account, tragedy once again involved a drug overdose, but in this case, the STE-er understood the importance of the after-death communication he received from his deceased daughter.

AN AFTER-DEATH APOLOGY EASES GRIEF

My daughter died of an overdose in 1998. She was my first-born and only daughter. We were extremely close. We had shared interests and hobbies, and we would spend many hours camping and fishing together. Both of us loved the outdoors and the environment. My daughter called me every Sunday night to see how my week had gone. As a father, I have experienced the close bond that develops with a daughter, but when she died, it was totally unexpected, and I had no idea she had developed an addiction.

Within an hour of her death, I heard her voice saying, "I'm sorry, Daddy." Her voice was as clear as if she had been standing beside me.

Over the following weeks, I was close to suicide. Then, one night I was camping, laying on my left side, when I felt a presence beside me. I then felt a hand on my right shoulder. As the presence began to leave, I once again heard my daughter's voice. She said, "I'm fine now. Don't worry anymore, Daddy."

I miss talking with her very much, but I now know her terrible battle and pain with drug addiction is gone. I have also come to believe in God and know he is in control.

A blessed apology from the other side eased this mourning father's grief and reassured him that his beloved daughter was just fine. Contact from deceased relatives does not relieve the grief-filled feelings they must experience in connection to missing their loved ones, but knowledge that physical death really is just a journey through the veil does quicken healing.

Not all overdoses need end in death, but when someone has a close call with their own physical demise, it can abruptly change their path in life. Such a traumatic wake-up call altered one alcoholic's life forever.

AN ENLIGHTENING EXPERIENCE

My name is Walter and I'm a recovering alcoholic. At the age of seventeen, I quit school and took up drinking. At the age of twenty-seven, I quit drinking and returned to school. In the early spring of 1962, as a member of the Royal Canadian Air Force, I was stationed at Calgary, Alberta, Canada. At the time, I was single and living in the military barracks in a room by myself.

One morning, around 3:00 A.M., I was awakened from sleep. The room was full of light, although it should have been completely dark since the light was off and the blind was closed to shut out any light from the outside. As I sat up in bed, standing before me was the most beautiful presence I have ever seen. Standing before me in the room was a Being of Light. The light radiating from the visitor began to engulf me as I experienced a most beautiful peace. Never before or since had I felt such peace and love. My first thought was, "Who are you? You are beautiful. Take me with you." I was ready and wanted to go with him right then. I knew it as a "him."

At this point, I honestly believed the "guardian angel" had come to take me away through a death experience. I felt extreme joy and happiness in knowing that I would be safe with this being.

The presence spoke three words and only three words to me. "Change your ways." These words were spoken, not as an order or a command, but as more of a loving suggestion, as if it were my choice to "change my ways." Then the presence vanished and I fell into a most peaceful sleep.

Upon awakening in the morning, my first thought was, "What a wonderful thing I experienced." Then, after a few minutes, my conscious mind clicked into gear and I started to worry about the visitation.

At that time in my life I was doing a lot of heavy alcoholic drinking. So I figured the visitor was there to give me a warning to "clean up my act" and "repent" because I was going to die soon.

I was scheduled to fly from Calgary to Lethbridge, Alberta in three days for a golf tournament, so I figured that the plane was going to crash and I would die. The visitor had come to give me a warning. I made the flight, won the golf tournament (while still drinking), and the plane did not crash.

After the flight, I still thought that I would die soon, so I "cleaned up my act" and stopped drinking. For twenty-six days. Then, a few months later, in June 1962, on a Sunday evening in daylight, while intoxicated, I had a near-death experience. I rolled my car, and as the car flipped over, I fell out of the car and it fell on top of me. The only thing that saved me from being crushed to death was that I was lying in a ditch. The next thing I knew, I was floating above the vehicle and looking at it from above. The first thought I had was that someone was pinned under that car down there. As I soared closer to get a better look, I was back in my body.

Shortly, a car stopped and two men lifted the vehicle off me and pulled me out from underneath.

I did not die in that crash. However, the result of that crash was that I spent three weeks in the hospital and exactly 100 days off work. The heart specialist told me that I had a cardiac contusion (heart bruise), and that I was very lucky to be alive.

Well, after that experience I made a decision to stop drinking again. After all, it would be insanity for me to drink again.

About two months later I was offered a drink. After thinking it over for a moment, the thought occurred to me: "One drink won't hurt me." So, against the heart specialist's recommendations, I started drinking again and continued to drink for another two years.

One evening while I was drinking a rye whiskey, a voice in

my head said to me, "Walter, that is your last drink. You don't have to do this no more."

I thought, "Well, if this is my last drink, I am going to enjoy it." I drank it and walked out of that bar. At that moment, all desire to drink left me instantly. That was my last drink. To this day, I have not had any desire whatsoever to take another drink. That day was October 7, 1964.

Update: October 7, 1997. I just arrived home from a meeting where I celebrated thirty-three years of continuous sobriety. What a wonderful thing to share with others—the gift of sobriety. For others, this is a testimonial that they, too, can go on living a rich and joyful life without having to resort to the use of alcohol, drugs, or other chemicals.

Aside from working with death and dying, Walter Collins went on to earn a bachelor of science degree in social work and a doctorate in religious philosophy. Walter, who is also known as Yashah, eventually trained at the Monroe Institute in Virginia, an OBE research center founded by renowned OBE experiencer and investigator Robert Monroe. Aside from writing more than thirty books, he has also worked extensively in the drug and alcohol counseling field for over twenty years. Today, he is dedicated to assisting those in spiritual need. Had Walter not experienced an STE brought about by tragedy, would he have touched so many lives?

This road called life has many twists and turns. Sometimes we travel emotionally to the heights of Nirvana, while at other stages of the journey, we feel trapped within the very depths of hell. Spirituality gives us a sense of balance as we move from one living adventure to the next. Knowing how to grieve the sad times is essential. Embracing the joy we meet is a must. Understanding that a good life lived involves both tragedy and bliss is the key to a spiritual path. In order to experience the ups, we must know the downs.

Our spirituality can carry us through the rough times and it can help us appreciate our blessings. When we experience STEs as a result of a tragedy, we receive the gift of unshakable faith. It is my dream that a day will come soon when those of us who have stepped into STEs can openly share our experience and strength with those who are in need of that added dose of faith and hope.

chapter nine

Dreamtime STEs— A Glimpse of the Other Side

Nothing is as real as a dream.

—Tom Clancy, bestselling author (1947–)

*A*ll of us dream. Dreaming is essential for mental and physical health. Most of our everyday dreams tend to rotate around desires or daily stress. Dreaming provides our mind with a way to discharge this tension and work out our living problems. As a mental-health provider, I know this to be true and often ask those I work with to journal their nightly romps through dreamland. Such information provides me with clues as to what might be at the base of my patients' emotional unease. Caregivers such as myself have used dreams as a springboard for exploring the inner workings of the psyche for centuries.

      ᐧ To the ancient Greeks, dreams had . . . significances as being nocturnal messages of the Gods . . . Dreams were . . . interpreted, in the Greek temples, as therapeutic indications, and their interpretations were recorded and used for medical purposes.[1]

Greek temples specifically built for dream healing were sort of like dream retreats, hostels, or hospitals. Dotting the coastal areas of the beautiful Mediterranean, these dream hotels were also known as Asclepion sanctuaries.

According to researchers Gertrude Toffelmeir and Katherine Luomala, the Greeks were not the only ones to use dreams to cure the ailing. Almost every ancient culture took dream material very seriously, including a curious group of Native Americans living in what is now called Southern California. These tribal people were known as the Diegueno. The holy healers, or shamans, within the community used dreams specifically for diagnosing and healing both psychological and physical illnesses.[2]

Yes, dream interpretation has been with us throughout history. But, unlike modern times, in cultures past the physicians and religious leaders of the time took them very seriously.

"Dreams were believed to be of supernatural origin, appearing in the form of visitations by . . . spirits of the dead, and at times beneficent agencies (angels, celestial beings). As prognostications of the future, dreams required a skilled interpretation. . . . Throughout Biblical literature, in fact, dreams were tantamount to prognostications."[3]

The Bible is one of the oldest pieces of historical literature known to humankind. Chock full of dream premonitions, the Judaic Tanach, or Old Testament, as known to modern-day Christians, consists of the Five Books of Moses, The Prophets, and The Holy Writings.

In the book of Job we learn how God can intervene on the sinful behavior of man by slipping into his dreams.

For God speaketh in one way, Yea in two, though man perceiveth it not. In a dream, in a vision of the night, when deep sleep falleth upon men, in the slumberings upon the bed; then He openeth the ears of men . . . (Job 33:14–16)[4]

According to this piece of scripture, during dreamtime, revelations and warnings are given to the individual who has fallen off the righteous path, so to speak. After some pretty frightening visions, the dreamer sees the light and corrects the error of his dishonest ways. In other words, a good nightmare can do wonders!

Predictions of the future are also common in biblical literature. In First Kings, we read how a loyal servant of God will receive many blessings.

ᔇ In Gibeon the Lord appeared to Solomon in a dream by night; and God said: "Ask what I shall give thee." (First Kings 3:5)[5]

King Solomon asked God for wisdom in ruling over his people. God was so impressed with Solomon's unselfish request (in that he didn't ask for wealth or long life for himself, or the heads of his enemies!), that not only did he give the king wisdom to guide his followers, he also gave him riches and honors, making him one of the greatest leaders ever to rule the land.

My favorite biblical precognitive dream is one familiar to anyone who went to Sunday school, and it can be found in Genesis 41. Here we have the tale of Joseph and the Pharaoh's dreams.

One night, the Egyptian Pharaoh had some rather unusual dreams. The interpretations he received from his court dream interpreters left him less than happy. Meanwhile, poor Joseph was sitting in Pharaoh's dingy, dark prison. The young man

spent his "jail time" interpreting the dreams of the other prisoners. One of these prisoners described Joseph's gift in Genesis
41:12–15.

> ∾ And there was with us there a young man, a Hebrew,
> servant to the captain of the guard; and we told him, and he
> interpreted to us our dreams, to each man according to his
> dream he did interpret. And it came to pass, as he inter-
> preted to us, so it was: I was restored unto my office, and
> he was hanged. Then Pharaoh sent and called Joseph, and
> they brought him hastily out of the dungeon. And he shaved
> himself, and changed his raiment, and came in unto
> Pharaoh. And Pharaoh said unto Joseph: "I had a dream,
> and there is none that can interpret it; and I have heard
> say of thee, that when thou hearest a dream thou can inter-
> pret it.[6]

The Pharaoh then shared his dream with Joseph and the
young man interpreted the vision as a warning from God of
things to come. Joseph examined the symbols within the dream
and then predicted seven years of abundance for the land of
Pharaoh, followed by seven years of famine. Based on Joseph's
interpretation of Pharaoh's dream, during the seven years of
abundance, Pharaoh prepared for the seven years of famine by
putting extra grain aside. Then, when famine struck Egypt, the
wise Pharaoh was prepared to feed his people, because Joseph
had basically socked away a great deal of grain in granaries
throughout the land.

Fast-forwarding from ancient culture to modern times, not
much has changed. To see how popular dreams are today, just
walk through a bookstore. Though traditional science tends to
turn its nose up when dreams are mentioned, page after page on

dream interpretation fills the bookstore shelves. Various philosophies and religions are used to justify these interpretations. Pop psychology is often mixed in with comical, far-fetched ideas about one of the mind's greatest mysteries.

Every author who has written a dream book is quick to announce that his or her interpretation of dream symbolism is the true key to understanding the self. Look at the following dream.

> ◐ A father had been keeping watch day and night beside the sick-bed of his child. After the child died, he retired to rest in an adjoining room, but left the door ajar so that he could look from his room into the next, where the child's body lay surrounded by tall candles. An old man, who had been installed as a watcher, sat beside the body, murmuring prayers. After sleeping for a few hours, the father dreamed that the child was standing by his bed, clasping his arm and crying reproachfully: "Father, don't you see that I am burning?" The father woke up and noticed a bright light coming from the adjoining room. Rushing in, he found that the old man had fallen asleep, and the sheets and one arm of the beloved body were burned by a fallen candle.[7]

When I read this dream, my immediate thought was, "What an incredible after-death communication." Here we have an exhausted father who collapses into sleep after caring for a beloved dying child. After the child has passed, an elderly guardian watches over the body while the grieved father sleeps. The child then comes to the father in a dream to warn him of a fire. Upon awaking, the words of the son hold true. A fire has indeed occurred. This particular after-death communication appears to be very straightforward. Interestingly, the author who recounted this dream was Sigmund Freud. Initially, I was excited to find such a dream reported by the famous analytic psychiatrist. But, my excitement quickly died a rapid death when I read the next paragraph of the account. Here is Freud's validation of another analyst's interpretation of this dream.

Complicated Psychoanalytic Dissection of a Simple ADC Dream

ᢍ The meaning of this affecting dream is simple enough, and the explanation given . . . was correct. The bright light shining through the open door on to the sleeper's eyes gave him the impression which he would have received had he been awake: namely, that a fire had been started near the corpse by a falling candle. It is quite possible that he had taken into his sleep his anxiety lest the aged watcher should not be equal to his task.

We can find nothing to change in this interpretation; we can only add that the content of the dream must be over-determined, and that the speech of the child must have consisted of phrases which it had uttered while still alive, and which were associated with important events for the father. Perhaps the complaint, "I am burning," was associated with the fever from which the child died, and "Father, don't you see?" to some other affective occurrence unknown to us.[8]

Whoa! After reading this, I just had to laugh out loud. This very confusing dream interpretation took me back to my years as a graduate student studying hard-core clinical psychology.

Oh, the long words, rationalizations, and overstated interpretations of the simple human experience! The above, typical, psychological analysis does not account for the vision of the child standing at the father's bedside. Along with this, the lofty assessment cannot adequately clarify the father's sensation of having his arm physically "clasped," nor does it offer a complete explanation of the verbal "reproach" he received from his son. It is a stretch to say that the child's complaints about a fever during illness provide an adequate explanation for the upset and concern the boy displayed in an ADC vision, over a fire that was taking place after his passing.

Reading books on dream interpretation can be interesting, but such dissections and categorizations of specific dream symbolism and one-sided understanding can leave readers confused and amused.

Just because an author has "Ph.D." listed behind their name does not necessarily mean their interpretation of your dream will be correct for you. In my own practice as a mental health-care giver, I often examine dreams, but what I might see in a dream might not "fit" for the person who has had the dream. This must be respected. Know that you are the best interpreter of your dreams. By journaling your nighttime visions, you can become your own "shrink," and you can learn a lot about your spiritual self.

Years ago, my dream journaling saved my life. I was violently ill, and the doctors could not figure out what was wrong with me. I then had a dream, which I believe gave me the answers. I dreamed worms were invading my body. In my night vision I saw tons of stringy creatures multiplying within my stomach. Upon waking, I went back to my doctor and asked if I possibly could have been infected with a parasite on a recent trip to Mexico. The first doctor wouldn't even listen to me and looked at me as if I had lost my mind. So, I went to another physician. Sure enough, test results proved I had indeed picked up a number of nasty "hitchhiking" gut worms while researching Mayan ruins on the Yucatan Peninsula. If these buggies had been left unattended, I could have ended up in serious trouble!

Old emotional hurts and wounds frequently surface in dreams, as do current concerns or fears. Nighttime visions can provide us with wonderful guidance as to how to proceed in healing ourselves from those painful life experiences, which are in need of our attention.

Dreams can also be a source of our creativity. The author Robert Lewis Stevenson was having difficulty writing a book and found his answers in a dream. This particular dream is at the basis of his famous work *Dr. Jekyll and Mr. Hyde*. In 1890, German chemist F. A. Keule had a dream that revealed the anatomical structure of the toxic chemical benzene. Today, there is much concern over this chemical's toxicity and impact on our health and the environment. I wonder just how many researchers realize that their knowledge and understanding about how to best deal with this chemical is based on dream material?

Though most of our dreams can be easily understood, every once in a while, our nighttime visions suddenly come alive with incredibly vivid scenes and inexplicable encounters. Renowned paranormal researcher and professor of psychology Charles Tart refers to some of these dreams as "lucid dreaming."

> Ꮞ Lucid dreaming is an altered . . . discrete state of consciousness characterized by the lucid dreamer experiencing himself as located in a world or environment that he intellectually knows is "unreal" (or certainly not ordinary physical reality) while simultaneously experiencing the overall quality

of his consciousness as having clarity, the lucidity of his ordinary waking discrete state of consciousness.[9]

Dr. Tart is right. After such intense, colorful sleep-time jaunts, most dreamers believe they have just taken an unexpected, quick trip to another realm of existence. Many experiencers are convinced they have visited distant heavenly lands and have communicated with deceased loved ones, angels, celestial beings, or higher spiritual powers. During such times, glimpses of future events are often encountered, and problems that seemed to have no earthly answer are suddenly resolved. As with the dream presented by Freud, disaster or difficulty can also be prevented with the help of an STE dream. If the father in Freud's account had not been awakened by the vision of his son, who knows what would have happened? Let's take a look at another interesting dream, one which is similar to that reported by the well-known father of psychology.

GET UP! GET UP! LOOK UNDER THE BED!

I was asleep in my bed. I had one child who was five years old. At 2:00 A.M., a woman's voice in my head clearly said, "Get up! Get up! You have to get up!" This voice woke me up, but I was confused . . . I got up and walked the house to make sure everything was all right. Not finding anything wrong, I went back to bed and fell asleep. Then again I heard, "Get up! You have to get up!" Again, I got up and walked the house. Confused, finding nothing wrong in the house, again, I went back to bed.

This time, while sleeping, I heard clearly in my head, "Get up and look under your daughter's bed!" The voice was very forceful this time. Immediately, I went to my daughter's room. Kneeling down, I looked under her bed to find that her pillow had slid down behind her headboard and was now lying on our baseboard heater.

As I pulled it out, I saw that it was burning, yellow flames in the center of it. Calmly and strangely unafraid, I carried the burning object, as if sleep walking, into the kitchen. I looked around, trying to decide what I should do with the burning pillowcase. Should I put it in the sink and turn on the water? Then I noticed that just outside my patio door, there was five to six inches of brand-new snow. So, I opened the door, stepped out onto the snow, and placed the burning pillowcase down and packed snow around it. Happy with my work, I went back to bed.

The next morning, I had no memory of the incident. None. It was just another normal morning. While sitting and having coffee with my husband, my eyes moved to the patio doors. Oh my God! The night before came crashing down upon me, hard. I then suddenly remembered everything! I told my husband what had happened, but after that, didn't talk about it for a long time.

I wonder how Freud would have interpreted the above, fantastic nighttime STE? "Who" called out to the sleeping woman in the dead of night? She could not see the burning pillowcase from her bedroom. The young daughter was asleep, unaware that her pillow had become kindling for a potential housefire, right under her bed. The husband was also deep in "zzz" land. In spite of repeated trips back to bed, for this woman, a good night's sleep was not in the cards. The unknown voice was persistent and was determined not only to get her up, but to have her look under her child's bed. How can such a warning be psychologically dissected or brushed off as coincidence or magical thinking?

Not all prophetic dreams bring frightening warnings. In an earlier chapter, we talked about pre-birth dreams. These STE encounters bring good news to parents-to-be. The following account is especially interesting, because the mother experiences a pre-birth dream about not just one baby, but two!

MY PROPHETIC "BABY" DREAMS

The dreams came to me four or five times over a period of about ten days in April 1982 and were remarkable for their vividness and their similarity. At that time, I was thirty-nine years old and had been married for almost sixteen years. My husband and I had been actively trying to conceive a child for more than fourteen years.

In all the dreams, I would be sleeping in my bed, when two small children, a boy and a girl about the same size and age, would come laughing into the room and tease me playfully until I awakened fully and agreed to get up. Then we would suddenly be transported to a beautiful meadow filled with lovely and fragrant flowers. The three of us would run and laugh and play; they would challenge me to a race, and I would always purposefully let them win—which they seemed to know, somehow. At the end of the race, we would grab and hug each other, falling to the ground and laughing merrily. Then the dream would end.

I don't usually recall dreams I have, but these dreams were so vivid; and when I woke up, I remembered every detail.

After I had had this same dream for the fourth time, I sat down and wrote about it in . . . a poem. . . . For some reason, I referred to the visions of the children as "ghosts," for they seemed such real persons, but I wondered, even at the time, if one could have visions of people who had never been born. Here is one poem:

Ghosts

They come to me in morning light,
Their voices sweet and clear,
And bid me leave my mournful night,
Their lips pressed to my ear.

So, from my bed, I rise and sweep
Them both into my arms,
And, glad to leave my dreamless sleep,
Surrender to their charms.

They lead me on a merry chase,
Through flower-scented fields,
And though I run a sturdy race,
They always know I'll yield.

Their childish faces, filled with glee,
Seem different every morn;
Can apparitions really be?
Of someone never born?

SMS—April 1982

It was only in retrospect, more than a year after Laura and Robbie were born, that I realized the dreams must have been prophetic in nature, as it seems so much more than coincidence that I had the dreams at the time Laura was conceived.

It is important to note that Saralyn's daughter, Laura, was adopted. Her dream coincides with the date Laura's birth mother conceived her. With this in mind, let's continue reading her amazing account.

In September 1982, I had decided to go ahead with major corrective surgery when I learned of an opportunity for us to adopt a child. I was working at that time for a group of attorneys, and I learned that a young girl had just come into the office to seek help in placing her yet-to-be-born child for adoption. . . . This baby was due to be born in early January 1983.

With this promise of a child, my husband and I decided that I would _not_ have the corrective surgery. We decided to go with the "sure thing" of an adopted baby, and began joyfully to prepare our home for the baby-to-be.

Early January came and went—and there was no word from the pregnant teenager. I began to despair that she had changed her mind. I began to have stomach distress—and I became quite sleepy in the office during the long afternoons, especially as I was not sleeping well at night. I attributed this to stress.

On January 19, 1983, my youngest brother, Don, who is a family physician, telephoned me from Pennsylvania to ask if the baby had been born yet. I explained sadly that the office had heard nothing further from the young girl, so I didn't know the status of the adoption—or even whether the baby had been born yet. Since I routinely shared my medical problems with Don, I told him how the stress was affecting my digestive system.

Don asked me a few more medical questions—and also learned of my sleepiness in the afternoons—and asked, "Uh, Sis, has it occurred to you that you might be pregnant?" I just laughed and laughed. How could I possibly be pregnant?

"But," said Don, "it wouldn't hurt to check, would it?" The next day, January 20, 1983, I was working at my desk when I received a call from my doctor's office. The nurse said that the test was positive and that I was pregnant

Hamp (my husband) and I were so elated—and so were a large number of our friends——that we all went out to a restaurant to celebrate. After lunch, as I walked down the hall toward my desk, I could see that there was a cake sitting on it. As our office always celebrated special events by having an impromptu party, I thought, "Oh, isn't that sweet! They're celebrating my pregnancy!" As I got closer to the cake, I could see that it was all pink—and it had the words, "Congratulations! It's a girl!" written on it. "But how do they know what I'm going to have?" I puzzled to myself. Then it hit me—my adopted baby had been born!

The girls in the office told me that it was no more than twenty minutes after I'd run out to tell Hamp of my pregnancy that they had received the phone call from the hospital saying my adoptive baby daughter had just been born! [News of] . . . two babies—and both on the same day.

And, as I said earlier, I completely forgot about the dreams I had had in April 1982, and the poems I had written, until a year or two after the children were born. It was only then that it struck me that God had sent those dreams to me at the time of Laura's conception; and it wasn't _me_ who had conceived, but Laura's birth mother.

And the dreams were so very vivid and explicit: there were always _two_ children, a boy and a girl of about the same age. I believe the dreams were God's promise to me that I would, indeed, become a mother and that I would have both a son and a daughter. Laura and Robbie will always be my two miracle babies.

These incredible prophetic pre-birth dreams foretold the birth of two babies! Amazing, isn't it? And this excited mother, Saralyn, learned about her arrival of her two babies on the same day! She would birth one beloved child in nine months, while another had already made entry into the world.

Saralyn's prophetic dreams were preparing her for big changes. Life is about change. A good life lived is never status quo. Sometimes these changes bring joy and celebration. Saralyn and her husband said, "Hello!" to two sweet little babies. At other times, change can mean saying "Goodbye" to someone we deeply care about. Prophetic dreams can ease the pain of such goodbyes and make grief a bit more bearable.

Below we have a true lucid dream. The experiencer fell asleep and then left her body, only to find herself visiting her deceased aunt in a beautiful garden. The aunt had several messages for her.

I COULD SMELL HER PERFUME

It was the night before Mother's Day 1999, and I had gone to bed rather late . . . I do not remember dozing off or falling into sleep. The "out-of-body experience" seemed to begin the moment I closed my eyes. I was on my aunt's old property. It was dark and gloomy. I stared at her empty garden and began to weep. My favorite aunt had passed away six years prior. . . . She had been an avid gardener in life, and her gardens were always brimming with flowers. I noticed my uncle's new wife playing with the dogs, but I was too melancholy to wave a hello. I just kept thinking how I wanted to leave.

I walked around to the side of the house, and as I rounded the corner, a beam of sunshine hit me. Warm and golden like the real thing. There it was, a beautiful garden that was so

breathtaking I have to struggle to find the words to describe it
. . . . I was in total awe. Behind me I could sense the presence
of another soul. I turned to see my Aunt Helen. She was
radiant, appearing almost ageless. Again I am struggling for
the right words. She smiled at me, and all I could think to say
was "you're dead, how can you be here?" To this she did not
answer, she simply held her smile. I then started to weep again
and asked her if I could touch her. To this she laughed and said
"yes." I will add here that I heard her voice in my head, not
externally. It was almost like she was communicating through
telepathy. I touched her hand and immediately fell into her
embrace. She felt warm, and I could smell her perfume.

When we let go she looked at me and said, "I am here
now" and pointed toward the garden. We began to walk
toward it, but I felt a barrier. It was not something I could see,
but I knew I couldn't go any farther. As my aunt walked farther
into the garden, she stopped and turned. She then spoke
these final words to me: "I know it's Mother's Day tomorrow,
and my children will miss me. Please tell them I love them."
That's when I came out of it. I was sitting straight up in bed,
tears running down my cheeks . . . yet oddly feeling both at
peace, totally refreshed, and exhilarated! It was so real.

Though I wanted to call my mother, it was 3:00 A.M., so I
forced myself back to sleep, and called my mom at a more
decent 7:30 A.M. My mother and I had a good cry that day.
She told me that me telling her about her sister was the best
Mother's Day gift she had ever received. Though my dream
lifted my mother, my aunt's message seemed solely for her
children. I did eventually contact all four of my aunt's children
and gave them her message. Each one privately thanked me,
and I hope truly believed in what I was telling them, but I was
still confused as to "why" I had had this visit.

Notice how full of color the garden is. This is very typical of STE dreams. Color is vibrant and often words, as we know them, are inadequate. This aunt was aware that Mother's Day was coming, and she wanted to ease her own children's grief.

I have carried messages from the deceased to their surviving family members on several occasions. What I have found interesting about these unusual spiritual requests is that family concerns do not end just because a loved one "moves on" to an afterlife existence. Old worries and relationship issues follow us to the other side! One deceased woman told me to tell her husband to just "Give it a rest!" She was very irritated with him and had grown tired of his continued complaining about a certain situation between the two of them. Her remark was very forceful!

Unlike my annoyed deceased visitor, the above experiencer's aunt lovingly told her to pass on a message to her surviving children. The aunt also had a message for her niece, but this communication from the afterlife didn't become clear until sometime later. In the following, we learn just what this message was.

AN ADC MESSAGE BECOMES CLEAR

I did eventually reconcile the "why me" question. Four weeks to the day I had the experience with my aunt, I learned my father was dying. . . . I believe my Aunt Helen contacted me that day not only to pass on a message for her children, but also to show me that the human spirit does transcend death. That we do go on, that our love carries on. At the time of my out-of-body dream experience with my aunt, my father seemed in excellent health. This is why I did not make the initial connection.

My father passed away on July 6, 1999. His death was sudden in that he lived only a few short weeks after a diagnosis of terminal cancer. . . . We had been determined to keep him out of the hospital and at home. My fondest wish at that time was that my dad could spend his final days within in his own bed and pass on in peace.

Before my father became ill, we had planned our family vacation for July. We were going to spend a week up at the cottage in the Canadian wilderness. When my father became ill, I told my husband to take the kids and go. I did not want to leave him. However, a few days prior to their departure, I sat alone with my dad. He questioned why I would not go. He said I looked so worn and tired. In fact, he insisted I go! "Catch a big fish for me, honey," he said. I didn't want to argue with him, and though I can be stubborn, I reluctantly went. The last words my father spoke to me were "give me a big smile, sweetheart, I love you."

We left on a Friday night, and on the Tuesday night, I stayed up late, sitting around the bonfire with my sis and my brother-in-law. We were gazing up at the night sky, which was magnificent . . . and talking about the wonders of the universe. I think that is when in my heart I knew my father was gone.

That night when I fell asleep I saw him. My father was sitting at a table; it had a white tablecloth and was laden with fine china and crystal, the type we could never afford. Each dish was filled with my father's favorite foods, steak, pancakes, and such. During the final weeks of his life, my father could not eat solid food. He looked up at me with a huge, wicked grin. "Look at all this food!" he said. He started eating again, then paused, and looking directly at me, he said, "You have a good life." He promptly went back to his banquet, and then I noticed the swish of a long gray skirt behind him. It was a woman, but I could not see her face. I woke up much the same way as I did with the other out-of-body dream. I felt as though I had been conscious the entire time and I could smell the food!

The following morning I already knew. I guess I wanted to prolong the inevitable, so I insisted we go hiking. When we returned, the proprietor of the bait and tackle shop in a nearby town was waiting for us. We had no phones, so I had left instructions at home to contact us if need be this way. The kindly proprietor looked grave. He was sorry to inform us that my father had passed away the previous day. I already knew. My dad had said his "Goodbye" to me the night before.

This is an extremely powerful STE. We have an after-death communication from a deceased favorite aunt. During this beautiful visitation, the aunt not only sends greetings to her children, but also lets her niece know life does not end with death. The niece, reassured that her aunt continues to exist in an afterlife realm, is subtly prepared for her father's upcoming passing. When her beloved parent does cross over, our STE-er then encounters a vivid departing vision and conversation with him. Both visitations occur during that ethereal, otherworldly experience known as dreamtime.

Saying "Goodbye" is so important. Often times, because of sickness or other circumstances, our departing loved ones cannot say farewell before passing. This often leaves surviving family and friends feeling as though "things" have been left undone. Our dreams are like highways, allowing us to travel from our world to other realms of existence. Knowing how to navigate these roads winding through the heavens doesn't take a degree in dream interpretation. Deceased loved ones seem to be very adept at making such journeys, and they make them often. It's as if they know these sleep-time visitations will soothe a grieving heart.

ONE LAST VISIT

I was half-asleep in my bedroom, at the back of the house, sunk in grief. Then suddenly I was seeing the kitchen, which cannot be seen from my bedroom. My mother came into the kitchen from the living room. She was wearing her pink and gray sweats, a favorite outfit.

She sat down on the stool where she always drank her coffee and did her morning crossword puzzle. She appeared to be trying to be very quiet so as not to wake me. I wanted her to stay, but I got this "strange" feeling that she was there just to look in on me one last time.

When we dream, our defenses are down. The daytime roadblocks society has erected against those experiences typically seen as unusual lose their hold on us when we drift off to dreamland. With the roadblocks lowered, the woman in the above account was able to catch her deceased mother checking in on her, mothering from the other side!

Knowing how to use our dreams to help us resolve here-and-now problems, along with past wounds, is not difficult at all. Learning how to navigate the dreamtime roads connecting us to our beloved deceased relatives, angels, or concept of a higher spiritual presence is also extremely easy. Here are a few tips.

1. Before going to bed at night, have a pad, pencil, and box of crayons by your bedside.
2. Set your alarm clock for anywhere between 2:00 A.M.

to 5:00 A.M.—"prime" dreamtime. This is a useful tip for those who don't recall their dreams in the morning.

3. If you want to make contact with a deceased loved one, look at a photograph of this person before going to sleep. Close your eyes and in your mind's eye, imagine asking this beloved individual to visit you during your dreams.

4. You can also meet up with spiritual guides or angels during your nighttime dream romps. Before going to sleep, close your eyes and visualize how you imagine your guide or angels to look. Ask them to come to you in your dreams.

5. Upon awakening, either to the sound of your alarm clock or the rays of sunlight streaming into your bedroom the next morning, pick up your pad and pencil and start writing about how you feel—uneasy, sad, glad, misty eyed, depressed, or elated—*before* getting out of bed. Next, if you can recall any dreams, write them down, too, no matter how strange they might seem. Some people find that drawing their dreams is also helpful.

6. After getting out of bed and finishing your morning routine, sit down with your pad and look at what you have written about your dreams. Ask yourself, "What does this mean to me? What does the symbolism of my dream say to me? What messages are being related to me?" Write down your answers to these questions. Trust your gut. Your first thoughts are usually the right ones.

With practice, you can become an expert at interpreting your own dreams. As you improve your skills, you will find that your nighttime visions become more lucid and adventurous. Eventually, fantastic trips to other heavenly realms of existence, foreknowledge of things to come, contact with deceased loved ones, angels, and spiritual presences will become second nature to you. Take a risk. Begin tearing down your roadblocks!

chapter ten

STEs Today and Yesterday—
History Continues to Repeat Itself

What lies behind us and what lies before us are
tiny matters compared to what lies within us.

—Ralph Waldo Emerson, American author, poet,
  and philosopher (1803–1882)

*W*hat spiritual essence lies within us? Philosophers such as
the American writer Emerson have been asking this
question for centuries and have yet to determine a conclusive
answer. Many famous thinkers refer to this mysterious inner,
ethereal core self as the soul. Words such as spirit, spark, consciousness, ideal nature, psyche, divine light, universal energy
force, and true enlightened being have also been used in an
attempt to try to define this elusive "Higher Self."

The major religions tell us the soul is not extinguished with
the death of the physical body. We are assured that, at death,
this divine spark of spiritual light flees the physical and takes
flight toward a new existence. If the soul cannot be destroyed,
if our consciousness can defy physical boundaries and escape
the confinement of skin, bone, and flesh, can it also reach out,
with invisible tendrils, and lovingly touch those we care for?

In order to understand STEs fully, we must destroy certain

societal myths and investigate just how connected to one another we really are. In order to begin grasping this new idea, let's begin this leg of our journey by looking more fully at the following account. After reading this, you will quickly see that the myth of separation at death is truly false.

I FELT HER PAIN

The thick gray fog, so common in the valley during the winter and early spring months, covered "The Raisin Capital of the World" with a blanket of thick mist. My grandfather, a first-generation Volga German, was mayor of Fresno, California, and raisins were our claim to fame. I had spent most of my young life in this town, just miles outside Yosemite National Park. Trapped in the valley by the surrounding High Sierra Mountains, the dense, misty San Joaquin soup could be bone chilling.

On an April afternoon, I bundled myself up in the ivy-green down jacket my favorite grandmother had bought me. Donning my much-loved string of multicolored "hippie beads," I pulled my waist-length blond hair out from under my jacket and made my way to the old Dodge Rambler waiting just outside my house.

Escaping the tentacles of the chilly fog, I slid into the back-seat of the car. Squeezing in close next to my girlfriends, our combined giddiness quickly chased the frigid temperatures away. We were off to see a Sly and the Family Stone concert, which was playing at a stadium near the center of town. This was my first rock concert, and the excitement of what was to come had captured my attention. In my mind I found myself singing Sly's bestselling hit, "Hot Fun in the Summer Time," but despite my surface glee, a small fear about leaving home tugged at me. For months, life at my house had been riddled with worry and sickness. Because of this, I had almost refused the invitation to see the concert. That cold afternoon, as the car drove off, along with the fear, I also had a twinge of guilt.

My thirty-eight-year-old mother was at home, upstairs, alone, bedridden, and extremely ill. At the age of thirty-three, she had been diagnosed with breast cancer. Treatment for this devastating illness bordered on barbarism during the late '60s. The surgery disfigured my beautiful mother, and the high-powered radiation treatments left her as limp as a willow. For five years she fought this disease, held it at bay, but now, like an enemy assault team, the cancer was rapidly making its way to every cell in her body.

At the tender age of fifteen, I suddenly became a surrogate mother for my two younger sisters. At this same time, I also adopted the role of mother's caretaker. If her hair needed coloring, I would gently brush the remaining tendrils and apply first the peroxide, followed by the ashen blond hair color. When my mother's nails required a new coat of paint, together we would pick a fun color of enamel, and then I would slowly apply the pink, orange, or red shade to each fingertip.

While attending to her needs, death was never, ever discussed. My blue-haired grandmother, who blotted out reality with red wine and Valium, had told me time and time again, "Just keep a smile on your face. Trust that God will save her. Don't say *anything* that would upset your mother." In spite of this attempt at positive thinking, I knew death was just around the corner, and I think Mother did, too.

Once at the crowded stadium, I found the shadows of cancer, illness, and death had receded into a corner, allowing me for the first time in months to truly be fifteen. Anticipation was mounting among the curious assortment of young people gathered for this major event. Denim bellbottoms and long hair, granny glasses and Earth Shoes were the required attire for this crowd. Periodically, a whiff of marijuana assaulted the nostrils, while on stage, the opening act was drumming out tunes at a deafening pace.

With blankets in hand, my girlfriends and I made our way to the center of the playing field, just yards from the stage. Spotting the cutest boys in school, we quickly laid out our fluffy blankets and plopped ourselves down next to them. After a bit of flirting, we heard the bad news from others sitting nearby. Once more, Sly was running late for a concert. It appeared the lead singer's well-known cocaine habit had gotten the best of him again and the show was going to be delayed by several hours.

As the D.J.s on stage began spinning the tunes "STAND" and "I'm Gonna Take You Higher," my girlfriends and I turned our attention back to the good-looking boys sitting around us. Batting eyelids thick with frost-blue eye shadow, we were bound and determined to be noticed by any cute teenage boy within a twenty-foot radius!

Our silly, flirtatious antics started out as great fun, until unexpectedly, I found I was beginning to feel very ill. Pain hit me from out of nowhere. A sickly feeling and weakness, which left me short of breath, engulfed my total spirit. Suddenly, flirting took a backseat, and without thinking, I found myself trying to get up. Where I was going was unknown to me. My girlfriends, now competing with one another for the title of "Hottest Chick in the Crowd," paid me little attention as I quietly moved off the pink, flowered blanket.

In the distance, I noticed a white ambulance parked near the entrance of the stadium. It was an old-fashioned station-wagon version, rarely seen nowadays. For some unknown reason, I found myself heading toward the vehicle. It was as if this ambulance was, at that moment in time, my one and only destiny. As unknown forces pushed me toward the automobile, I noticed I was beginning to feel even weaker than I had while sitting on the blanket. Making my way to the old ambulance, my whole being was now focused on reaching the mattress inside. Once I attained my goal, I crawled into the back bed of the vehicle and fell soundly asleep.

After several hours, I awoke to discover the concert was over. In spandex and glitter, Sly and his band had finally shown up. Feeling just fine, I sat up to find two sets of blue frosted eyes staring back at me. They were not happy. I crawled out of the warm cocoon of the ambulance as my frightened girl-friends looked on with great concern. While zipping up my green jacket and running my fingers through my now very tangled hair, confusion gave way to anger as my companions sarcastically said, "We have been seriously scared stiff! We didn't know where you were." This was then replaced with a bit of genuine concern as they asked, "Are you okay? You look just awful!"

Once my two buddies realized I was perfectly fine, anger returned. "We spent the whole concert looking for you! How could you do this to us? Sly came on for just a few songs and then he was gone!" As I wiped the remaining sleep out of my eyes, I looked back at the bed in the ambulance and wondered, "What just happened?"

The trip from the stadium to my front door was eerily silent. No one was talking to me. With crossed arms and the periodic agitated toss of long hair, my girlfriends took turns glaring at me. In spite of this, I was totally disconnected from the strong emotions seething through the car. Instead, I sat perplexed, wondering why had I just spent several hours in the back of an ambulance?

After I climbed out of the backseat and the car sped off, I walked up to my front door. The fog had thickened, and at that moment, I "felt" something just wasn't right. Crossing the threshold into the house, my mother's visiting nurse greeted me with tears. Sadness engulfed my entire home. Racing up the stairs to my mother's blue bedroom, I quickly saw the light blue bed comforter had been tossed onto the dark blue shag rug on the floor. My mother was nowhere in sight. With panic, I grabbed my mother's nurse and asked, "Where is she?"

Over the next several hours I was to hear how earlier that afternoon, my mother had suddenly felt very sick, weak. Her breathing had become labored and the visiting nurse had called for an ambulance to take her to the hospital. Initially upon hearing this, I did not connect it with the strange turn of events I had experienced that afternoon at the stadium. My concern was for my mother's well-being. Would she live, would she die? Sadly, just days after being whisked away from our home on Sharon Street, my mother died alone, across town, at the young age of thirty-eight.

Several weeks after her passing, I lay down on my bed in an attempt to sleep. Her death, the funeral, and the many family dramas that had accompanied this hard time had worn me out. In the solitude of darkness, I began to replay my afternoon at the concert in my head. As I focused on how ill I had been feeling, enlightenment struck. My unexpected spell of physical distress had occurred at approximately the same time my mother's nurse had called for the ambulance. Sitting up in bed, astonishment hit me like a typhoon.

My unforeseen illness at the concert had not been an accident. The abrupt bout of sickness had begun to batter me at the exact moment of my mother's own sudden, severe physical suffering. The denial of the "unusual" finally lifted. I was at last forced to admit I had made my way to a parked ambulance at the stadium just as my mother was being loaded into an ambulance sitting in front of our house. With incredible clarity, I recognized Mother and I had shared a very powerful connection. Though miles away from home, I had experienced with my mother the beginning stages of her physical death.

The above experience might sound very unusual, but in actuality it isn't that uncommon. This is a type of deathbed or departing vision (DBV) known as an "empathetic DBV." Though rarely discussed openly, such encounters have taken place time and time again throughout history and continue in modern times.

During an empathetic DBV, a family member, friend, or even healthcare worker will actually feel, emotionally or physically, the same things a dying person is experiencing. As life begins to end, surviving individuals can experience the similar symptoms of illness or physical distress encountered by the dying person. The empathetic DBV can occur even when there are miles between the dying loved one and the family member or friend. Curiously, the same thing sometimes happens at the beginning of life, when a loved one or friend of a pregnant mother feels sympathetic birth pains as the mother delivers a child. For a brief moment in time, there is a psychic connection.

How common are encounters of this nature? They happen so frequently that the "movers and shakers" in Hollywood have used them as major movie plots to entice moviegoers into theaters. STEs are frequent enough to have made it into popular culture, but they are not just the product of science fiction movies and books. Well-known popular media personalities have also been personally exposed to this phenomenon.

Jack Lemmon, the celebrated actor who starred in many

fine feature films such as "The Odd Couple" and "China Syndrome," witnessed an empathetic DBV early in his life. It happened when he was an undergraduate at Harvard University.

JACK'S TALE

I was just twenty-one and going to college back East and had a close friend. We were playing tennis one afternoon when my pal was suddenly stricken with feelings of dizziness, nausea, and most of all dread, for no apparent reason.

I managed to get him home, and just as we arrived, so did a man from Western Union with an emergency telegram. My pal read that his mother had died suddenly. She was some 2,000 miles away in the Midwest. She hadn't been sick, so her death was a complete shock. It turned out that she died at exactly the time my friend had suffered from those terrible feelings.[1]

As a passing nears, can we experience the same emotions and physical sensations our dying loved ones meet? Are we all psychically connected? If we were to believe history and religion, it would seem so. Let's revisit the afterlife beliefs of the major religions and see what it is they have to say about such powerful STE encounters.

Connecting Visions in Religion

For the Jewish people, a strong sense of religious and cultural interconnectedness comes from the holy book of Torah. The conviction of most religious Jews is based on the words contained within the five books of Torah. Recorded by Moshe

Rabbeinu (Moses) at Mount Sinai and believed to come directly from HaShem (God), the Torah connects all Jews, down through the ages, throughout the world, to one another and to their God.

Jewish mysticism fully embraces the STE experience. The Zohar (which means radiance) is the most famous of classic, mystical interpretation of the Torah. Written in Aramaic, this Jewish book of mysticism is purported to be the teachings of a second-century rabbi named Shimon ben Yohai. According to legend, while hiding in a cave for thirteen years in an attempt to escape persecution from the Romans, the Zohar was revealed to Rabbi Shimon. The prophet Elijah, accompanied by his angels, presented words of revelation about the meaning of life and life after death to the rabbi.

Interestingly, the Zohar isn't really mentioned in other historical Jewish writings until the thirteenth century. At this time, supposedly, a Spanish Jew named Moshe de Leon discovered the mystical text. It was after this that the Zohar, or Book of Splendor, was published and circulated to Jews throughout Europe. The words of the Zohar are a rich source of historical information on Judaic mysticism, especially as it relates to belief in an afterlife.

Down through the centuries, Kabbalists, or Jewish mystics who studied the Zohar and followed its teachings, truly believed that when the Angel of Death came knocking, a glimpse of the afterlife realms would be offered. Within this tradition, mystics practiced a variety of meditation techniques to prepare for such transcendental experiences. Utilizing visualization, meditation, specific doctrines for lifestyle, ritual, and prayer, Kabbalists expected periodic messages and revelations from the world beyond.

The serious student of Jewish mysticism did not view

visions of deceased relatives, angelic beings, or visionary guides as unusual. The Zohar actually instructed followers not only to expect such experiences, but to share these encounters openly with those dying and at the deathbed. It was strongly thought such sharing would validate for the dying and those at the bedside the understanding that death and separation were just an illusion.[2]

The Rebbe Mystics

"Hasidic (a form of Judaism founded in the mid-eighteenth century in the Ukraine) literature abounds with stories describing the deathbed experiences of many Hasidic rebbes (another word for rabbi). These stories are often very detailed and show how many rebbes made the transition from life on the physical plane with a sense of equanimity and calm. There were some rebbes able to describe the visions they witnessed as death approached. In the hour before he died, Shmelke of Sasov saw his deceased father, Rabbi Moshe Leib, and his great teacher, Rabbi Mikhal of Zlotchov, standing beside him."[3]

Students of the Zohar have read time and time again how the deceased relatives of a dying man will visit him as his own death draws near. "Thus, the Zohar teaches that 'at the time of a man's death he is allowed to see his relatives and companions from the other world' (1,219a). Similarly, 'we have learned that when a man's soul departs from him, all his relatives and companions in the other world join in and show him the place of delight . . .'"[4]

It is important to remember that the Zohar is a historical work that was written many centuries ago. In modern times, when a passing approaches, visions of deceased relatives not only continue to be widespread, but are similar to those described by the ancient rebbes.

Many current DBV accounts are parallel eighteenth-century stories. Similar descriptions of life-after-death visions come from those at the deathbed of a loved one. Modern-day experiencers often report seeing "something" leave the body at or near the moment of death.

IS SHE GONE?

August 4 . . . is a day I will always remember. We were told Mom was near the end. I remember walking from the kitchen to her bedside to join the others who were present that day. We then began praying the Rosary out loud, while holding hands. At this point, we weren't praying for her to get better. We were just praying, praying for her passage, or as she use to say, her journey.

At that moment, I saw a fine mist descend down over her. Mom then opened her eyes, looked up, smiled, and left, as did the mist. I then asked, "Is she gone?" "Yes" was the answer. . . .

No one said a word at that time about what we had just seen. Later, while talking to my sister about Mom's passing, I asked her, "Did you see anything strange?" We both had the same vision, down to the same exact details regarding the cloudy mist coming down and then, after her passing, ascending. My brothers and husband were also able to confirm the vision. They had seen it, too. We all agreed Mom hadn't just taught us how to live. She had also taught us how to die."

Here is another similar modern-day account.

WISPY AND WHITE

My mother went into the hospital . . . and soon fell into a coma. . . . The night of her death, I went home around 10:00 P.M. and fell asleep soon after. My husband could not sleep and was watching television in our bedroom, as I lay beside him. My husband explained the following account to me.

He said that at about 12:30 A.M., he saw a "form" of a cloud, wispy and white, come into our bedroom. . . . The "form" or cloud hovered over me for a brief time, then floated through the bedroom and connecting bathroom to my two daughters' bedrooms. After this, he saw it go back down the hall.

Twenty to thirty minutes later, we got a phone call from my father, telling us that my mom had passed away.

Centuries ago, powerful STE encounters convinced the Jewish mystics that death was not to be feared, separation from loved ones was but an illusion, and consciousness was not extinguished. Today, the modern STE-er is learning the same lessons. Throughout history, witnesses to the deathbed STE have recognized that death is just the departure point for an adventurous journey from one level of consciousness to the next, closer to God. The mystics understood that physical death relieves one from the bondage of separation. For the modern-day experiencer, what was true then continues to be true today.

Christianity and the DBV Experience

Greek Gnosticism, which greatly influenced early Christian doctrine, was based on the strong belief that the human soul was a divine spark of God. Followers of this faith alleged this godly glow was trapped within the physical body. This condition created a separation from God. With this disconnection, it was believed the soul had forgotten its true identity. Salvation from a sense of separateness could only be experienced once the soul achieved "gnosis" or knowledge of the true self. Recognition of the true self could occur with experiences of enlightenment. For many Christian martyrs and saints, this enlightenment came in the form of otherworldly visions.

As we saw earlier, serious scholars are aware that the Gospels contained within the New Testament of the Christian Bible confirm that Jesus predicted his own death on more than twenty different occasions. Predictions of an upcoming death are often dismissed by skeptics as coincidences or natural consequences to particular situations occurring in the environment, with politics, or one's physical health. In some situations this might be true, but then there are those precognitive experiences that are rich in detail and difficult to explain away.

I believe Jesus had numerous, profound STEs before his actual crucifixion. These precognitive visions prepared him, both spiritually and emotionally, for the painful journey he would travel as death neared. His physical death, followed by the after-death communications and visions experienced by his followers, continues to connect Christians across the globe. A little over a century after the death of Jesus, another student of the Christian code would have a powerful precognition about his own upcoming demise.

St. Polycarp had been a student of the original disciples of Jesus. As a result of this, he then spent his entire life preaching the Christian gospel, and eventually he became a Christian bishop. In his late '90s, Polycarp was still attempting to turn people away from pagan practices and toward the teachings of Jesus. The Roman authorities were less than pleased with the bishop's activities. They eventually threatened him not only with the loss of his wife and family, but with death if he did not refrain from preaching. Polycarp stood tall against the mighty Romans, but his followers and friends did eventually persuade him to go into hiding. During this period of concealment, the bishop spent most of his time at prayer. Three days before his capture by the Romans, Polycarp had a powerful vision. During his STE, he felt as though the pillow under his resting head was on fire. Based on this experience, he came to the stark realization that he was to face death on a flaming funeral pyre. The bishop knew intuitively that he was to be burned alive. Polycarp then shared these prophetic visions with his followers.

After he was captured, the Romans demanded he renounce Jesus as Christ, but instead, Polycarp announced he was a Christian. When he then refused to honor Caesar, his funeral pyre was erected. As the flames grew higher, those witnesses present said Polycarp's flesh refused to burn, and in response to this, he was pierced with a Roman dagger.[5] Based on an STE, the Christian bishop was able to predict with incredible accuracy just how he would leave this world.

Part of Christian doctrine is founded on the supposed visions and resurrection of Jesus of Nazareth. Followers of this religion strongly assert that physical death is not the end and that separation is but a myth. Reunions with departed loved ones living an afterlife existence are readily accepted and expected. For centuries, the followers of Christianity openly acknowledged STEs such as angelic visitations, near-death experiences, prophetic dreams, and after-death communications. With the turn of the nineteenth century and the continued scientific advances of the twentieth century, visions of an afterlife were relegated to the status of old wives' tales and uneducated superstition.

Sadly, today both Christianity and Judaism typically regard STEs, along with other related experiences, as byproducts of either mental illness or fanciful thinking. Many clergy members are not educated about the STE and are quick to dismiss those accounts reported to them by their congregants. Some sects of Christianity see such visions as the consequence to a lack of faith or the influence of the devil. Likewise, unaware Jewish leaders often insinuate such accounts are not a part of Judaism, and this can leave the Jewish experiencer feeling very confused and abandoned.

These shaming interpretations of the STE can create fear for those who have had an encounter of this nature. This lack of understanding on the part of the clergy often perpetuates a sense of spiritual separation.

The Hindu Religion—an Eastern Perspective

Unlike the West, Eastern religions continue to look with interest upon visitations from the unseen world. The Hindu religion tells us the Atman, or the core self, is never separated from the Brahman, or godhead, and that individuality is but an illusion. In Sanskrit, enlightenment, or Moksha, means release from the cycle of reincarnation. Moksha is the process of waking up from the dream, which tells believers they are separated from one another. With Moksha, one finally merges not only with others, but also with the cosmic Brahman. A traditional image of this merging commonly used by Hindus is that of a droplet of water falling into the ocean and becoming one with the sea. In 1948, a very well-known Hindu and political leader experienced a connectedness with not only Moksha, but with time and space.

Mahatma Gandhi Predicts His Own Passing

Precognitive STEs about future events defy time and space. As we have seen, many STEs have precognitive components. India's Mahatma (which means Great Soul in Sanskrit) Gandhi encountered episodes of precognition that prepared him and his followers for how he would die.

Mohandas Karamchand Gandhi (1869–1948) was a lawyer, religious Hindu, and much-loved nationalist leader in India. Following World War I, this quiet man worked diligently with passive resistance and nonviolent means to establish his country's freedom from Britain.[6] Sadly, not everyone in India was content with his success. The morning of his death, Gandhi foresaw his own assassination and told his attendant Manubein: "If I die . . . somebody shot at me and I receive his bullet on my bare chest, without a sign and with Rama's name on my lips, only then should you say that I was a true Mahatma . . ." Gandhi had a strong suspicion that he would be killed—the accuracy of his prediction is uncanny. On January 28, two days before his death, Gandhi told Manubein: "If I am to die by the bullet of a madman, I must do so smiling. God must be in my heart and on my lips. And if anything happens, you are not to shed a single tear."[7]

Earlier that morning, his faithful servant had asked Gandhi about preparing cough drops for him. As a result of his most recent fast, Gandhi was suffering from a cough.

 confirmed On the morning of the 30th, as Manu was preparing some throat lozenges for the night, Gandhi chided her, "Who knows what is going to happen before nightfall or even whether I shall be alive? If at night I am still alive you can easily prepare some for me." That same morning, Gandhi told a coworker to "bring me my important letters. I must reply to them today, for tomorrow I may never be."[8]

On January 30, 1948, while attending another prayer meeting, a mad assassin named Godse shot Mahatma Gandhi in the chest and abdomen three times, at point blank range. Gandhi's predictions about his death and the exact manner in which he would die continue to spark a sense of awe for the Western world at large. Gandhi was seventy-eight years old.

With investigators such as myself, STEs in the form of predictions, empathetic experiences, visions of deceased relatives, or any otherworldly encounter are not seen as a new phenomenon. We understand such experiences are as old as time itself. For centuries, it was commonplace for the grieving to look to the visions and precognitions of the dying for reassurance that physical death would not separate them from loved ones. Because of the strong belief in STEs, death was not seen as the end.

Every major religion across the globe has a belief in some sort of afterlife existence. After death of the physical body, most belief systems contend the essence of life continues in an unseen world. As a death neared, the ancient Egyptians would begin reciting certain prescribed formulas and holy names to ensure the dying person's spirit would travel safely to an afterlife existence. After passing, the recitation of these formulas continued. The Egyptians believed that at death, one would eventually receive an Oahu, or new body. With the Oahu, they could then enter the Field of Rushes (a type of Egyptian heaven).

For the Buddhist, death brings a quick glimpse of the joy that is to come once all incarnations have been completed. The ecstatic vision of "clear light" occurs at death, and the intensity of this light supposedly increases with each incarnation. The ultimate goal for the Buddhist is Nirvana, or a transcendental loss of self.

According to the Islamic holy book, the Koran, a good life will eventually lead to a place in Paradise or al-Jannah. In Paradise, there is a garden, which has been prepared for those who have followed the law of Islam. In this garden, all sorts of delights await the true seeker.

∾ Tribal shamans of both the North and South American Indian cultures utilize ritual practices of various forms to guide departed souls from this life to the next. For the true Native American, death should not be approached with trepidation, but is seen as a natural progression toward further spiritual adventure and development. For followers of the Bahai faith, physical dying is a happy time, a time for Happy Release.[9]

The Bahai religion is not alone in its positive, hopeful presentation of life after death. The philosophies and historical writings devoted to major religions strongly suggest physical death is not the end, but a new beginning. Religious history also tells us that the visions of the dying and of those at their bedside are a normal part of the transition from this level of existence to the next. Throughout history, STEs have assisted the dying in preparing for their upcoming physical death. These beautiful encounters have also reassured countless remaining loved ones that life continues.

As death drew near, certain ancient Jewish sects viewed visitation from the Angel of Death as a positive encounter. In centuries past, Christians greeted glimpses of heaven, angels, and deceased relatives with joy. Just 100 years ago, premonitions about an upcoming death gave those who were soon to cross through the veil a chance to tie up loose ends, heal old rifts, and provide reassurance to remaining loved ones that relationships continue. Our ancestors eagerly "listened" to communications delivered from otherworldly messengers. Sadly, our devotion to the "god of science" has put an end to this. Today, when with the dying, if a message is given, many in society are quick to put cotton in their ears.

Look, Listen, Be Aware

In December of 1999, popular movie actor Jack Lemmon played the role of a lifetime in a television movie called *Tuesdays with Morrie*. The program was based on the bestselling book of the same name, by Mitch Albom in 1997.[10] The book was based on the last days of a seventy-six-year-old Jewish college professor's life. Dying of Lou Gehrig's disease, or ALS, Morrie Schwartz openly shared with Mitch Albom what the dying process was like on a physical, emotional, and spiritual level. This brave soul publicly taught all of us how to pass with dignity.

For Lemmon, the experience of playing Morrie was timely. In a statement to *The Orange County Register* in December of 1999, here is what Lemmon had to say:

> ∾ "To a certain extent the movie is bound to make you think of your own mortality and what you've accomplished,"

Lemmon said. "A number of times Morrie would have a line of dialogue and I'd think afterwards, "Boy, I hope I'd feel that way when my time comes."[11]

Approximately eighteen months after the television movie aired, Jack Lemmon, like the man he played in the film, passed away at the age of seventy-six. Was his last major television movie role, that of a dying man, a mere coincidence? Or was it an STE preparing him for his own afterlife journey, which was just around the corner? I would like to believe that as Jack Lemmon immersed himself into the role of a dying man, he also took the time to remove the cotton from his ears and was, on some level, listening to a message from an otherworldly messenger.

Experiencing an STE before a passing can initially be over-whelming, especially if we are not prepared for such an encounter. Encountering STEs after a loved one has moved on can be equally bewildering. Instead of using these encounters to soothe our grief, many of us tuck them away and rarely share them for fear of ridicule from society. Let's take these beautiful otherworldly experiences out of the closet and see how we can use them not only to ease our grief, be to reassure us that we are all truly connected.

chapter eleven

STEs—A Soothing Balm for a Grieving Heart

"It is the nature of humanity to mourn for the loss of our friends; and the more we loved them, the more poignant is our grief."

—George Washington, first U.S. president (1732–1799)

*G*rieving is normal. Every time we lose something, be it a job, our health, financial security, our youth, a relationship through a breakup, divorce, or a lifestyle change, such as children growing up and leaving home, we need to grieve. We must grieve the loss of what was, because more than likely, it will never be the same again. If we are to survive the many bumps and bruises life often offers up, knowing how to understand feelings and deal with grief is essential not only for our emotional and physical health, but also our spiritual well-being.

When a loved one dies, grief takes center stage. Even when physical death ends terrible agony and suffering, our grief cannot be ignored. My friend, author and lay minister Ron Wooten-Green, had this to say about how our lives change when a loved one dies.

"All of a sudden, we must relearn the world around us. So

much of our world is defined through the existence of a significant other. When that person leaves our life, much of the world, as we know it, also leaves. . . . With that person's death comes a need to redefine who we are. Grieving then requires a process of learning all over again how to relate to everything and everyone in our world. It also requires a relearning of our relationship with the deceased person as well. All of this relearning takes time—a lifetime."[1]

Yes, even our relationship with those who have passed on changes. How many people actually put aside the time needed to grieve losses, and the changes they bring, completely? Take a moment and think back to the last funeral you attended. Chances are the funeral bouquets were fragrant, the ceremony was beautiful, and the eulogy was endearing, but the public displays of tears was short lived. After the funeral service or trip to the cemetery, family and friends of the deceased most likely gathered together at a restaurant or someone's home. Good food was eaten, funny stories about the departed were shared, a few more tears trickled down cheeks, but caution was taken not to say anything that might upset the closest family members.

Because Western society is very "death phobic," concerned friends and family typically do not know how to talk about death to the grieving. Our culture teaches us to fear death, not talk about death. Society spends many dollars to keep the dying alive for just a bit longer, and when death finally does arrive, a sense of failure permeates the air.

Instead of understanding when it is time for ill loved ones to "move on," people often say, "The doctors did everything they could to keep him alive, but it just wasn't enough." If the death is sudden, excuses for the passing are quickly made to justify untimely death and tone down grief. "Well, for the thirty-eight years she was here, she lived a very full life. It was her time to go. God needed her." These words were spoken to me after my own mother's death, and at that time, this statement told my sixteen-year-old mind that the intense grief I was feeling was wrong. How could I be sad if God needed my mother?

Once physical passing has happened, death and anything related to coffins, cemeteries, or cremation is quickly brushed under the rug in a matter of months. The rationale is, "If we don't talk about it, the feelings of hurt, anger, loneliness, confusion, and abandonment will go away!"

Justification for the inability to know how to grieve or emotionally assist the grieving is often exhibited as follows: "We don't want to upset her, so be careful about what you say. Her husband died so quickly and you must watch your language. Don't talk about how he passed. Don't use the word death. Don't mention the cemetery. You might make her cry." Sadness, normal sorrow, sobbing, and anguish over the loss of loved ones are behaviors minimally tolerated in our culture.

Pulling oneself up by already stressed bootstraps and keeping strong emotion in check are often seen as positive reactions to a passing. "Look at how together he is! He is doing so well! Laughing, telling jokes, and his wife died just six months ago. I hear he hasn't shed a tear. We need to keep up the positive talk! It would be terrible if he fell apart now!" Society sees the behavior of the recently widowed man in the above example as "healthy." However, such behavior is a mark of trouble to come. Unexpressed grief can follow people throughout a lifetime and often impacts physical health. Free-floating depression, anxiety, spiritual difficulties, hidden anger, nightmares, difficulty in relationships, and a host of physical ailments can be directly tied back to buried grief.

In our culture, people often see open grieving as a sign of ill health, emotional weakness, or even self-centeredness. Loud wailing, intense fury, deep despair, numbness, and the need to withdraw frightens many people. Because of their own uneasiness with the forceful expression of feeling, others might literally attempt to quiet down those who are grieving. In response to death, periodic tearing up might be accepted, but long-term, "natural" sadness, rage, suffering, depression, and the need for isolation are often seen as abnormal. "She sure has been crying an awful lot. She locked herself in her bedroom yesterday. He died a month ago and she should be better now. Have you thought about referring her for medication?" These are typical comments I often receive from family members concerned about the grieving loved one visiting my office for grief therapy.

When the public display of tears has dried up, family members assume that mourning has passed. As one man said about his wife's grief over the recent death of her sister, "Thank goodness she has gotten over that! I couldn't take the crying." This was far from the truth. The wife hadn't stopped grieving, but she now hid her tears from her husband because she knew he disapproved.

One woman shared with me that her friends were surprised to see her grief return on her departed husband's birthday, three years after he had passed. "They actually thought his birthday would no longer affect me. Am I abnormal? Is there something wrong with me for feeling sad?"

If grief continues for more than several months, apprehension from family members and friends can erupt. "What? Why should you be sad? It's been a year. Get on with your life. Your loved one is in a better place now, and you should be happy he isn't suffering. He wouldn't want to see you crying and upset. Think of your children. Your tears are frightening them. Pull yourself together. Be strong for them."

Such comments are made to the grieving all of the time!

Imagine how relieved these individuals feel when they learn that hard grief can last for several years after a death and that such grieving is perfectly normal.

Anniversaries, holidays, and special events can bring grief to the surface. It is also important to note that children will only feel comfortable grieving if the adults around them are able to grieve in a healthy, healing manner. After my mother's death, my grandparents tucked their grief away. As a result, when sadness about my mother's death would hit, I would immediately think something was wrong with me.

Eventually, I discovered my grandparents were at fault, hiding their pain behind glasses of wine. My grief was normal, and learning how to feel it was essential. When I graduated from college, got married, and had children, the grief I had about my mother's early death returned. During such moments, it was important for me to find a quiet place and have my tears. After acknowledging my sadness, I would then close my eyes, visualize my mother, and tell her just how much I missed her. Before my wedding, when I had desperately wished she were there pinning the flowers on my veil or at my bedside, holding my hand while witnessing the magic of birth, I had to feel the loss of her physical presence in my life. At times, I have even written letters to my mother about my grief.

This grieving never takes longer than ten to fifteen minutes, and afterwards, I always feel better, clearer, and more at peace. Acknowledging a passing allows us to release the feelings associated with loss. Letting grief flow through, as opposed to blocking or stuffing it, is the key. When we do this, when we allow ourselves to grieve, we then make room for a new type of relationship with the departed, one that reaches across the abyss, separating this life from the next. Today, I might periodically grieve the "move" my mother has made, a move from this life to another reality of existence, but I also know that when I really need her, she is here for me.

When I recognize I'm experiencing grief, I will take quiet time to embrace it fully. Too many people push grief away. I did this for years. Forcing grief underground only increases its power. It takes a lot of energy to keep such strong emotions at bay. By giving myself permission to sit quietly and feel my sadness each time it arises, I can slowly let go of grief. Listening to soft music, journaling, painting, or just visualizing what I am sad about, like the passing of a beloved family member or friend, enables me to feel my losses fully and then release them. In this way, grief can flow on through and I can return to living life in the here and now.

Unaware Family, Friends, and Professionals

If a grieving or dying individual experiences an STE in the form of a deathbed vision or after-death communication, family, friends, clergy, and healthcare workers will often refer to these encounters as grief-induced hallucinations. Here are some common misinterpretations of STEs: "She is so distraught about her son's death. Now, she imagines he visits her! Can you believe it?" or "What are we going to do? As Pop's death nears, he talks more and more about being visited by his deceased sister. We should talk to the doctor about putting him on medication to control these delusions." When it comes to STEs, medication is not the answer, but many professionals continue to see this as the solution. Currently, if STEs are reported by the dying, the prescription pad frequently materializes and doctors dole out strong tranquilizers or antidepressants.

Instead of supporting STE encounters, using them to assist the grieving, reduce fear of death, soothe sadness, and heal loss, unaware loved ones and helping professionals, more often than not, quickly dismiss these spiritual gifts. With action and so many words, they let the grieving person know future discussion of such "woo-woo" events will be relegated to the category of delusional thinking. As one elderly eighty-something-year-old woman said to me just the other day:

∾ For years I have received visitations from my family members right after they have died. For me, this has been just wonderful. It eases my pain. My loss. I know for a fact that death is not the end, and though I feel sad and grieve that we can't visit more often, I understand that when my time comes, all my family on the other side will be there. My son the doctor says I only imagine these visits, that it's just a byproduct of my grief. Brain physiology he says, but I don't think so. It's so hard to talk to people about this. They don't understand.

Society must move toward accepting the STE phenomenon. Instead of downgrading these magnificent experiences to that of superstition, mental illness, or overactive imagination, people must begin to see them as real and as a healthy, healing part of the living experience. An STE can positively alter the entire course of our lives. The following is a perfect example of this. Bette Killion, bestselling author of children's books, recently sent this incredible departing vision to me. She has written numerous books for youngsters with wonderful titles such as *Thinking of It* and *The Apartment House Tree*. Bette had read about my investigations into departing visions in my book *One*

Last Hug Before I Go: The Mystery and Meaning of Deathbed Visions and felt compelled to share her husband's account with me. Here is William's STE.

GRAMPIE AND THE APPLE TREE

When I was just seven years old, my grandfather became seriously ill. I had always, from my very first memories, been very close to him and I called him "Grampie."

The first morning I found he had taken to his bed, I went to his door and stood there shyly until he beckoned me to come near.

"Don't be afraid," Grampie said. "All is well."

He then reached out and touched my face.

At that same moment, one of my aunts had just arrived. She saw me and then quickly shooed me away. Over the next three days, this was the way it always went. Though another aunt came to stay and everyone was in and out of Grampie's room, being a young child, I was not allowed to visit him.

Because my mother was so busy, I didn't want to try to ask her questions. As for my aunts, outside of a few sweet little pats on my head and the continual need to shoo me away, they didn't seem to want to bother with me.

I often took refuge in my favorite apple tree at the edge of the orchard. There was a little place among the limbs built just for me. Sitting here, I could see the leaves above me moving in the sunlight and patches of blue sky far up. To a small, confused boy, they were like flags of hope.

On the fourth day of Grampie's illness, I had escaped as usual, to my tree, when suddenly I was aware of a presence moving toward me from the house. I have never been able to adequately describe it. "It" was an all-white form. To my young mind, this white form looked as though it was made of the cheesecloth my mother used to strain berries, yet it was filmier, more elusive.

This white filmy form floated straight toward me in the tree, hung for just an instance very near, and then slowly drifted away—off above the trees and into the clouds.

I watched until it disappeared. Strangely, I was not afraid. Instead, I just felt a great sense of wonder. I then quickly climbed down the apple tree and ran to the house. My mother met me at the back door and clasped me in her arms.

"Grampie just died," she said.

At the moment of his grandfather's passing, while sitting in the fragrantly scented branches of his hideaway, this innocent young child encountered the otherworldly white form of his grandfather's departing spirit. For William, there was no sense of fear. When the loving essence of his beloved Grampie stopped by the apple tree to say goodbye, the little boy felt only a sense of awe. Young William was given a peek at what is to come once life, as we know it, ends.

Many years later, this vivid memory provides the elderly William with a certain understanding that death is not the end, but a mystery to look forward to. When relieved of the fear of death, people can truly live life, and William has done just that.

Having spent several decades aiding individuals healing from loss, I often hear breath-stopping, descriptive, vibrant accounts of otherworldly visions. Visits from deceased loving relatives, celestial beings of intense light, and glorious views of a world beyond the veil ease the transition from this life to the next for the dying and make grief bearable for those left behind.

Over the years, I have received countless departing visions

by mail, e-mail, and word of mouth, not only from the dying, but from family members and friends. Along with this, a few brave doctors, nurses, and clergy members have stepped forward to share STE encounters. Each has a story to tell—a gift to offer. After reviewing close to 2,000 STE accounts related specifically to the death of a loved one, I can say without hesitation that this is not a unique experience to be found only in the headlines of supermarket tabloids.

German, Spanish, Greek, Japanese, Jamaican, American, British, and Eastern European people, individuals from every socioeconomic group imaginable, have spoken to me about their precious death-related STEs. These experiences come from people of all walks of life. Young, old, religious, not so religious, Christians, Jews, Buddhists, and Muslims, those who are religiously befuddled, and even atheists, have shared similar accounts. Prior to their STE encounters, most of the experiencers I have talked with knew little about the New Age movement or literature discussing such topics.

Most of the individuals who present their amazing accounts to me are initially fearful about talking openly. Many have already encountered eye-rolling ridicule and are leery of being referred to as crazy or accused of having an overactive imagination. After recognizing that I am truly interested in hearing what they have to say, these brave souls take a deep breath, relax, and pass on just a bit of what they have experienced to me. With great wonder, joy, and amazement, they intimately share fascinating and profound, life-altering glimpses of an existence science has yet to begin exploring. As the years have passed, I have found myself becoming more dedicated to investigating these wondrous visions, especially with regard to how such encounters assist in healing grief.

Death is not the end, and the STE departing vision not only

eases grief, it also alters understanding of what happens once the physical body gives out. Here is a remarkable after-death dream communication.

HE WON'T NEED THAT LITTLE RED BAG

I grieved terribly . . . when my friend revealed that he was HIV positive, that is until I decided to enjoy every minute with him while I had him with me. I was privileged to be at his bedside when, after a brief devastating illness, the decision was made to unplug his respirator and allow him to die. On the way home from the hospital, I was amazed at how exhilarated I felt.

Three nights later, someone at the door awakened me from sleep. I went downstairs, and here was my friend, carrying his little red athletic bag. He came in, sat down on the piano bench, and began talking. I was dumbfounded and kept thinking, "You are dead. We buried your ashes yesterday."

He talked about how wonderful it was to be well again, and then said he wanted to go upstairs to talk to my husband, who was still in bed. When he came downstairs, he said, "Don't worry. We will be together again in the next life." He then took me in his arms, hugged, and kissed me. Then he left.

I ran upstairs and said to my husband, "Did you see that? He was really here!" My husband then said, "Yes, but he won't need that bag where he's going." Then I woke up and cried, for the first time since my friend's death. The experience was so real. . . .

What a wonderful friendship this was. How fine it is to know that love transcends death. When a friend experiences a death in their circle, sometimes I'm now brave enough to ask if they have had visitations in their dreams.

I have shared the above account with not only mourners who have lost a loved one to AIDS, but with those diagnosed with this terrible disease. In the above account, the experiencer has a classic ADC dream. Her deceased friend comes to her in a nighttime vision, looking happy and well. Reassurance of a reunion is given and goodbyes are said. No longer ill and physically wasting away, this beloved friend then leaves for the next leg of his afterlife journey. Dreams of this nature feel very real and have a profound impact on the experiencer, one that stays with them throughout a lifetime.

Taking these astonishing death-related STE accounts out of hiding and placing them squarely into the lap of the individuals who have lost a loved one or who are, themselves, preparing for physical death lessens the fear of the dying. When the fear of death loses its grip, then the real work can begin. The real work involves preparing for change.

Though these beautiful visions can comfort the dying and those they love, STEs do not rid surviving loved ones of the "I will miss you" emotion. This is a normal response to the physical separation death creates, regardless of whether or not someone believes in an afterlife existence. For the STE-er, the blow grief gives is different. There is an understanding that life continues, but the relationship has changed. This change in the relationship must be grieved. Once this is accomplished, there is then an unquenchable thirst for knowledge about religion, the paranormal, and other spiritual topics. Avenues for dealing with the "new" relationship between the living and those existing in an afterlife realm are explored.

Along with this, STEs dramatically reduce the influence a very popular twenty-first-century scientific notion has had on many of us. Traditional science would have all of us believe physical death is the end. For the STE-er, such philosophy no longer holds true. Departing visions suggest the long-held medical, materialistic perspective on death might just have a few loop-holes. As more and more STE-ers come forward, it will be very difficult for science to continue to deny the positive impact these otherworldly visions have on the dying and those who love them. The following account clearly demonstrates the positive effects STEs have on the dying and their family.

A PEACEFUL DEATH

I lost my mother about a month ago from breast cancer, and before she passed . . . she did have deathbed visions. She was in the hospital and the doctor told us that there was nothing more they could do for her. He (the doctor) gave her two weeks to two months to live . . . One day, while in the hospital, she was looking up at the ceiling, and my dad, noticing this, asked her, "What are you looking at?" She responded, "I'm looking at eleven white things." With this, my dad asked, "Are they angels?" And my mother quickly answered, "Yes!"

My mother was in her right mind. She never did need to have any drugs to keep her comfortable. For some reason, God spared her any pain.

We decided to take her home and have hospice come in. For two weeks we asked her daily whether or not the angels had returned. Each time we asked, she replied, "No, I haven't seen them."

One evening, my dad and my sisters were sitting on each side of her bed. My mother suddenly looked at my sister and said, "Boo? (This is my sister's nickname.) Who is that standing behind you?" There was no one standing behind my sister.

On the Wednesday before she died, my mother started

reaching out in front of her. She was fully awake during this time. We asked her if the angels were back, and she said, "Yes!" My brother then asked my mother if the angels were talking to her, and once again, she replied, "Yes!"

Mother went into a coma the next day and died twenty-four hours later. I do believe she was seeing angels. As I said earlier, at that time, she was in her right mind. Also, it is important to share that initially my mother was very afraid to die, but after seeing what she saw, she was at peace with everything. She also said she was going to be fine, that she was going to a much better place. How could my mother tell us this if she hadn't received a glimpse of where she was going (after she passed)?

I was so at peace when she died. I knew she had become an angel herself and had gone straight to heaven.

Let's explore the content and positive effect the above experience had not only on the dying woman, but also on her family. First of all, this ill mother informs her family that she is seeing "eleven white things." She is very specific and descriptive. Her daughter then makes it clear to us that her mother was "in her right mind" at the time of the vision. The dying woman also, without hesitation, validates her husband's question, "Are they angels?" with a "Yes!" This, too, is passed on to other family members. Thankfully, the adult children in the family are open to hearing about their mother's visions. Sadly, thanks to the scientific dogma regarding death, this is not a typical response from most family members.

In recent history, STE visitations have been discounted by the scientifically minded and clergy alike, relegated to the category of hallucinations and delusions. I, for one, believe such pat answers miss the mark altogether. Medical professionals are often quick to tell the grieving, confused family of the dying, "These visions are totally physiological in nature." Even when medication is not used and the cause of the passing is in no way interfering with thought processes, medical personnel, clergy, and even mental-healthcare providers are hasty to dismiss the death-related STE vision.

Though these reported visions might appear as only empty space to us, we must recognize that our loved ones, our dying friends, or patients are seeing something or someone. During such times, as opposed to tossing these otherworldly gems aside, we need to follow the example of the family in the above scenario by actively listening, learning, and, if appropriate, by asking the dying questions.

As is typical of such STE encounters, in the above account the angelic visitors didn't create distress for the dying woman, but instead were readily accepted. Visitations such as this are a core component for many of the STEs I have investigated. Visions of loving deceased relatives, angels, or celestial beings can play a major role in soothing the individual who is fearful of dying. After encountering a vision, a once combative, fearful, angry person, confronting his or her own imminent passing, suddenly calms down, lightens up, looks forward to physical death, is freed of fear, and even shows concern for grieving loved ones.

The soon-to-pass individual, having the STE vision, will often seem confused that no one else in the room can see dead "Uncle Joe," "Grandmother," or the team of angels standing by the bedside or in the corner of the room. This confusion can be misinterpreted as fear, and unaware family members and professional caretakers can become concerned for the sanity of the dying.

As I said earlier, the family in the above example is unusual. Instead of questioning the mother's mental state, they were interested in the visions and wanted to talk openly with her about them. The visions not only assuaged the fear of death for the dying woman, but they also comforted surviving family members.

Those at the bedside can also become concerned when the dying suddenly start talking about taking trips or begin lifting their arms up to some unseen vision in the room. Because the dying person seems to be reaching out to something tangible, confusion can once again set in for family members who cannot see with the naked eye just what it is their loved one is grasping for. As a dear lawyer friend of mine reported:

"Just before passing, my father looked to the ceiling, sat up in bed, and with a joyous smile on his face, lifted his arms up, toward someone only he could see. While in this position, he beamed with delight, gently fell back onto his pillow, and then passed peacefully. It was one of the most remarkable things I had ever seen in my life. He looked so peaceful, and I know he had been visited by someone who had come to help him to the afterlife."

As the veil between this world and the next begins to part, to whom are these departing loved ones reaching? When we die, are we greeted by loving relatives and friends living an afterlife existence? Can we scientifically explain these visions away, or do we need to come to terms with the fact that there is more to the physical dying experience than meets the eye? What about the survivors, those at the bedside of the dying? They, too, encounter visitations, visions. Are they also "just" hallucinating? If not, shouldn't we also be listening more closely to them?

Finally, what do these visions tell us about life after death? Do they really provide us with a glimpse of the next level of reality, or is this just wishful thinking? Are these STEs an illuminating, vivid preview of the journey we will all take when we experience the spiritual wonder of passing from this life to the next? How can we break through the denial of STEs, which has been perpetuated by medical science? The answer is clear. We must seek out experiencers from within the helping professions.

Unseen, otherworldly visitors don't just say "Hello!" to the dying. Those of us who are caring for a soon-to-be departing family member, friend, or even patient might also sense a spiritual presence or receive full-blown, "Here I am!" visitations from departed friends or relatives. Recently, I received just such an account from Mike Tymm, board of trustee member for the Academy of Religion and Psychical Science and editor of the *ARPA Bulletin*.

> Dear Carla,
>
> I don't watch John Edward's popular television show [John Edward is a very well-known medium who claims he is able to contact the deceased, living in an afterlife reality] much anymore, but I caught his show today. At the end of the program, one of the guests said that her mother was very frightened of death. She also added that she was there when her mother passed. She said she saw her deceased father enter the room and beckon to the mother. The mother then left her body and told the daughter there was nothing to it. It was a very credible account. I wish I had taped it.

Like the dying, a few caretakers have also encountered detailed, brilliantly colored scenes of heavenly landscapes. Angelic apparitions have brought comfort to a number of professionals. Often, healthcare workers encounter beautiful, Technicolor lucid dreams that accurately predict an upcoming death and are accompanied with an added message that "All will be well" from a deceased relative, friend, or patient. Unfortunately, many nurses, doctors, clergy, and mental-health workers are still unprepared for STE encounters.

The visions of the dying often frighten unaware healthcare providers. Fear of the unknown perpetuates more fear. May professionals also have difficulty knowing how to respond to an STE. This uncomfortable unease is a byproduct of our culture's current lack of understanding when it comes to the STE encounter. I believe all caretakers need information about the departing visions of the dying. Awareness reduces fear, and when fear is lessened, comfort increases.

Thankfully, there are some caretakers who are very familiar with STEs. Their familiarity with such encounters enables them to normalize the experience for dying, confused family members.

IT'S NOT A HALLUCINATION

Having spent the last twenty-eight years in the "Helping Professions" as a critical care nurse and therapist, I have not only heard of patients seeing lost loved ones, but have felt their presence. . . .

I have heard patients ask to have a family member called because they have a special message for them from a family member who has already passed over, and they want to convey this before they lose it. And they become furious if you tell them they are hallucinating, it's just the pain medication, they just think they are hearing something, or to just rest and the voices will go away. The voices don't go away, and if those at the bedside have the courage really to listen to the dying person, they will reap rewards. . . .

I recall one dying woman who was full of infection. Because of this, she was alone, in a room; no one was allowed to visit her, and no one wanted to care for her. She was the worst assignment you could pull in a shift because her care was so consuming and she was very uncomfortable and demanding.

She would grab my hand and say, "Did you hear that? Tell my husband I need to talk to him. His mother is here and wants to tell me something. It's about that piece of land he wants to buy. Go get him." We called him and explained to him that his wife might be hallucinating, but when we mentioned she was talking about his mother visiting and saying something about some land he wanted to buy, he returned to the hospital. He arrived at her bedside in about thirty minutes, and his wife passed ten minutes later.

I saw the husband about three weeks after her passing, when he stopped in to thank us for calling him one last time. I asked him if the things his wife had said had any validity to them, and he went pale. He told me the information he had received from his wife was correct. He then added that what was most fascinating was his wife gave him information only his deceased mother knew about, no one else. This information involved things that his mother had kept secret between him and her. Hearing these secrets from his wife told him this was truly a message from beyond.

Here we have a seasoned healthcare worker who is very familiar with the departing visions of the dying. A message from a deceased relative is being relayed through an ill woman who is preparing to leave this world. As physical death nears, she appears to have one foot in this existence and another in the next. Because this critical care nurse suspected her patient had an important message to share, she trusted her experience and called the woman's husband.

The message from the husband's deceased mother contained private information that the dying wife had no way of knowing. She could only have heard about it from her husband's mother, and the mother was deceased. While alive, the mother never shared this information with her daughter-in-law. Since the nurse acted quickly, the husband was able to hear this message from his deceased mother just moments before his wife passed. This experience validates for him that both his mother and wife will be together in the afterlife.

Most STEs encountered by helping professionals typically deal directly with the person passing and his or her loved ones. Every so often, healthcare workers are themselves the direct recipients of messages from the dying. In the following account, a nurse receives a personal visitation.

I HAVE GROWN SPIRITUALLY

I have worked with so many dying patients over the last few years, and I have experienced so many things that have helped me grow spiritually. . . . A [dying] woman spoke of beautiful women, all in white, wispy, flowing gowns, referring to them as angels.

One man described people all in white, waiting in long lines. He also mentioned that his mother and sister were in the room and waiting to take him home. . . . My most memorable moment was when this same man told me that there was a man in white who came through a door, which I could not see. He said he didn't know who he was, but that his name was Charlie. I asked his wife, who was at the bedside with me, if they had ever known anyone by that name, and she said no.

I had recently lost my grandfather, and his name was Charlie. That would have explained the extremely eerie feeling I had at that very moment. It still sends chills up my spine.

The last one I want to tell you about involved another gentleman who was on his deathbed. I can pretty much tell how much time a dying person has left in this world, because

I have been exposed to death and dying for so long. This man was very near his departure from this life. His family came to spend some time with him, and his minister was also visiting and praying with them.

I was in another room and suddenly felt this little brush across the back of my neck, along with an unusual feeling. Then, the dying man's daughter came to get me to come back to his room. That was the same moment the dying man took his last breath. . . . I realized he had passed by me, on his way to the afterlife, to let me know he was going.

All of my experiences have given me a spiritual understanding that an afterlife exists and that nobody here will understand it until we get there ourselves.

Did the nurse's recently departed grandfather come to visit her by way of her dying patient's vision? How do we explain the "eerie feeling" she had at the time of the vision? And what about the "brush" she felt on the back of her neck as the dying man took his last breath? Those who have encountered an STE often share that such experiences have been accompanied by unusual physical sensations. When visited by my deceased loved ones, physically seeing these relatives in spirit form, I noticed a drop in room temperature. They also reached out and touched me, and I felt this touch. As our nurse with twenty-eight years shares, "At the bedside of a dying patient it is most common to feel a cold spot in a particular section of the room. No matter what you do, it won't warm up. . . ." Sensing a presence without actually seeing just who is visiting is not an uncommon experience.

When working in a care-taking role, it is not unusual for bonds to develop between professionals and patients. These bonds of friendship often continue after a passing has occurred.

MY FIRST DEATHBED VISION WITH A PATIENT

I worked for hospice for three years. . . . I never regretted doing it for one minute. I had a deathbed vision with the first patient I had.

We knew his time was getting close, but did not realize just how close. I was scheduled to go to his house at 9:00 A.M. So, I set my alarm for 6:00 A.M. in order to get up and ready. For some reason, I was in one of the deepest sleeps I'd ever been in. I tried to wake up, but felt like I had been drugged and couldn't wake up. Then I started dreaming, or so I thought.

In the dream, there was a man lying on a bed with his eyes closed. He then said, "I just came to say goodbye." I said, "Who are you?" He then said, "You know who I am."

I said, "Oh! Okay! I know who you are now!" Then he said, "I just came by to say goodbye." I replied, "No! Please wait for me to get there." He then said, "I am sorry, but my time to go is now, and I cannot wait."

I replied, "Well, okay. Goodbye then. I'll see you again someday."

Then I woke up, but had a hard time getting up and motivated. I was running behind schedule when . . . the phone rang. It was my patient coordinator, calling to tell me that my patient had died around 6:00 A.M. that morning. I was shocked beyond words. I knew we had formed a bond, but never realized how much of one until that moment. [She then ends the account by thanking me for my work with departing visions and adds she will share this with her "believing" friends.]

This patient wasn't about to take off until he properly said goodbye to the nurse who had cared for him. Somehow, he was able to find a way to connect with his caring nurse one last time. During deep sleep, are we able to enter other realms of existence? If so, just how is this achieved? What about the STE visions experienced while wide awake? Is our brain like a radio antenna, capable of tuning into different realities of existence? And if so, just where is this physical antenna located? With regard to this complex question, near-death researcher Melvin Morse, M.D., shares these thoughts.

Tuning In

Does the human brain create visionary experiences, or does it receive them telepathically in an area of the brain where the material and the spiritual worlds meet?

This is a sticky question, because it can be fairly answered either way. After examining thousands of case studies and even after having had a death-related vision of my own, I can say without a doubt that the brain both creates visionary experiences and detects them. There seems to be a huge area of the brain that is devoted to having such experiences. Just as we have a region of our brain devoted to speech and one that helps us regain our balance when we trip and almost fall, we have an area that is devoted to communication with the mystical. It functions as a sort of sixth sense. In short, it is the God sensor."[2]

If Dr. Morse is right, science has a great deal of work to do. And if research can prove that we do have a sixth sense, then science will have a series of problems to address. How does our sixth sense reach out to other realities of existence? Can we learn how to "tune in" to other dimensions and make contact with our loved ones who have moved on? What do these other dimensions look like, and where are they?

One internationally known theoretical physicist, Michio Kaku, has already begun exploring the physics behind parallel universes. In his book *Hyperspace* Dr. Kaku goes into great detail about how other dimensions beyond our own can exist. His groundbreaking theory, hyperspace, provides for parallel universes.

At one time, the scientific community looked upon such theories with great skepticism, but today, modern physics is actively exploring the possibility of other universes coexisting with our own. When I'm swimming in the ocean, I often see brightly colored fish darting in and out of the reef, but what I don't see are the billions of magnificently shaped microorganisms feeding all around me. Because I cannot see them with the naked eye, does this mean they do not exist? No, they do exist, but I would need a microscope to see them. It's the same with the possibility of parallel universes, and modern physics is currently investigating this. At present, we are lacking the tools to see other dimensions, but that does not mean they do not exist.

Imagine what our world would be like if science could prove that our loved ones do not cease to be once death has visited them, but instead move on to another plane of existence. Like the invisible microorganisms feeding off the reefs, I believe our loved ones are out there, just a breath away, in another world, parallel to the one we are living in. In time, classes devoted to developing our sixth sense could become as common as reading, writing, and arithmetic. Until that day, we must be willing to open our minds and listen to the experiences of those who have had STEs. If we ourselves have had an STE, we must pass our wondrous accounts on to those who are willing to hear us. With just a bit of motivation to learn, a whole new world can open up to us.

chapter twelve

Living with an STE—
The Integration Process

"We had arrived . . . two extraterrestrials in
a very foreign land."

—Dr. Edgar Mitchell, astronaut, scientist, and author (1930–)

*A*s we have seen, everyday people from all walks of life are
regularly encountering STEs. Once touched by an STE,
existence as we know it is often changed forever. Our views on
spirituality, the environment, priorities, and our relationships
with others are radically altered. Integrating this new awareness
into our everyday living experience can be quite a task.

Moving past the feeling of being alone in our experience is
often the first roadblock we confront. Upon visiting my office,
most experiencers want to know just how common STEs are.
According to a recent June 8, 2001 Gallup Poll analysis,
Americans' belief in psychic and paranormal phenomena is up
over the last decade.[1] Belief in psychic phenomenon must be on
the increase for a reason. Are more and more STE-ers acknowledging their encounters? Hopefully, yes. While STE-ers are far
from alone, connecting with other like-minded people can be a
great challenge.

Because experiencers are finally speaking up, STEs are also slowly making their way into the field of medicine. A recent Dutch study, involving the prevalence of NDEs among cardiac patients, was published in one of the world's most prestigious medical journals. According to *The Lancet*, NDEs are more common than once thought. Three hundred forty-four cardiac patients were interviewed upon resuscitation. Sixty-two of these patients reported NDEs.[2] That's over one-sixth of this group. How do you connect with people such as this? Where can you find them? You must begin by sharing your account with others. Those of us who have come forward with our own STEs have discovered we are not alone. We have found ways to seek out other experiencers and create a network of support. In my own search, I found one seeker who has been paving the path for the rest of us.

Edgar Mitchell, a graduate of MIT, with a doctorate in astronautics and aeronautics, is best known as the astronaut who piloted the lunar module for Apollo 14 to the moon. Dr. Mitchell is one of a select few who have stood on the moon's surface and looked back in awe at the small planet we call earth. One might think that the experience of walking on the rough, silent, dusty surface of the moon would be enough to produce an overwhelming STE encounter. Interestingly, Dr. Mitchell was more profoundly affected on the flight home.

CONNECTEDNESS AND A NEW BEGINNING

It wasn't until after we . . . were hurtling earthward at several miles per minute that I had time to relax in weightlessness and contemplate that jewel-like home planet suspended in the velvety blackness from which we had come. . . . It was all there, suspended in the cosmos on that fragile little sphere.

What I experienced during that three-day trip home was nothing short of an overwhelming sense of universal connectedness. I actually felt what has been described as an ecstasy of unity. It occurred to me that the molecules of my body and the molecules of the spacecraft itself were manufactured long ago in the furnace of one of the ancient stars that burned in the heavens about me. And there was a sense that our presence as space travelers, and the experience of the universe itself, was not accidental, but that there was an intelligent process at work. I perceived the universe as in some way conscious. The thought was so large it seemed at the time inexpressible, and to a large degree still is. . . .

By the time the red and white parachutes blossomed in the life-giving atmosphere of earth three days later and our capsule splashed into the ocean, my life's direction was about to change. I didn't know it then, but it was. What lay in store was an entirely different kind of journey, one that would occupy more than thirty years of my life. I have often likened that experience to a game of pick-up sticks; within a few days my beliefs about life were thrown into the air and scattered about. It took me twenty years to pick up those sticks and make some kind of sense of it all, and I now believe I can describe it with an adequate degree of comprehensibility and scientific validity.

. . . After leaving NASA in 1972 I founded the Institute of Noetic Sciences in California. This would fund much of the scientific research that I wanted to see accomplished to help me better resolve the complex insights from my experiences in space. Since then the institute has thrived. . . ."[3]

Dr. Mitchell's STE encounter drastically changed the course of his life. Over the last several decades, he has been committed to investigating human consciousness and psychic and paranormal phenomenon. The Institute of Noetic Sciences has been a major part of this famous astronaut's journey. Mitchell's ultimate goal is to find common ground between science and the spirit.

Even for an astronaut, having an otherworldly experience can be an earth-shattering, soul-blasting, mind-blowing experience. Moving from feeling overwhelmed, confused, and fearful of sharing to not caring what others think can be quite a distance to travel. Like Dr. Mitchell, after an STE encounter, experiencers often discover a second roadblock. Belief systems of the past no longer match up with the sudden bombardment of new spiritual awareness. Old lifestyle pursuits, such as the quest for material wealth and fame, lose their grip and are replaced by a different set of priorities. After being socked with an STE encounter, change is inevitable, and this change is often difficult.

The one time workaholic, who regularly spent hours away from the family while at the office, slaving away day and night for the almighty dollar, suddenly realizes money isn't everything. As the result of an STE, time with the family becomes a new, top priority, but the family has learned to live life without him. His re-entry into the family creates power struggles, and a period of adjustment to "Dad being home more often" is needed. The big paycheck abruptly takes a backseat, and though our seeker might be willing to give up the cushion of success, those around him have learned to depend on it.

For the individual caught up in a destructive relationship, an STE can provide quite an awakening. With an STE, the fog of confusion is lifted. The lights are turned on, reality hits, and the courage to say, "This is my life, I'm going to live it as I see fit, and I will no longer put up with your need to control or abuse me!" unexpectedly comes bubbling forth. Such boundary setting is often followed by a painful period of time alone. This period of "relationship drought" is often necessary for self-examination in order to determine "why" self-destructive relationships have been so attractive.

Many addicts and alcoholics have begun the road to sobriety after experiencing an STE. An STE encounter filters through the haze of intoxication and provides the addict with an other-worldly moment of clarity. This moment of clarity is often accompanied by a preview of a sober life. Sobering up after living life in a chemical haze involves months of relearning how to live clear and awake to reality. Such times can prove to be most frustrating and painful. Looking at the havoc drugs or alcohol has created, and then taking responsibility for this, can be overwhelming.

For those who are fearful of dying, because of the prospect of nonexistence, an STE encounter often eradicates all-consuming feelings of death anxiety. After such awareness, a spiritual "high" can take hold. Concerns then turn to being of service to others who are truly hurting or are in need. Unfortunately, in the process of carrying the new spiritual message, the seeker often forgets to take care of everyday needs. Learning how to balance out the needs of others with the need to care for the self can prove to be frustrating.

Once glimpsing heaven, the nonbeliever becomes a believer in powers greater than the self. An unquenchable thirst for spiritual growth begins. Such growth rarely takes the form of a clear-cut path. The man in the following account began his spiritual journey with the passing of his beloved father. Rob Delaney's dying father's departing vision ignited within him a desire to open himself up to the unseen world, but with each answered question came a host of new ideas to consider.

THE JOURNEY BEGINS

With great trepidation I write, as I still find it hard to explain the DBV I had with my father back in 1997.

Dad was terminally ill with brain tumors and was not on any medication at all, as he did not experience any physical pain from them. Nothing was "blurred" by prescriptions.

Three days before he died, he explained that my mother and my sister, who had both passed years before, were at the foot of his bed and had been asking him to come with them. My immediate reaction was to ask him if he would like to go with them. (As I knew death was imminent, I felt giving him permission might ease his passing.) He decided, and told me, that he wasn't ready yet and had told them so. They went away, only to return the next day, and were, according to Dad, quite persistent that he come with them. He said "there were others" there, too, but didn't name them.

Upon this second visit and after consulting with the family earlier, I told Dad that if he wanted to go with them, at any time, that we had all agreed that he didn't need to ask us for permission, he had it all along, and that we'd be fine and could take care of ourselves.

The morning of his death, I was with him and my sister at his bedside holding him when he passed away.

I must say that hearing my Dad's DBV with my own ears and seeing with my own eyes, I felt an incredible sense of relief knowing about DBVs. My own mortality has been reassured of where I might be going and that I'm not going to be alone! I actually found the process fascinating and have started reading more about it, comparing notes with many friends and coworkers who have experienced this themselves. . . .

Obviously, your research has shown you countless stories like this, and I thought you might like to hear just one more.

My own personal research into dream study and my experiences with family members who have passed over has been startling for me. As one who has no religious background whatsoever, it has certainly got me asking a lot of questions. Can you suggest any readings about contact or messages or what I would call "life lessons" that I keep getting in my dreams from loved ones? (These are conversations that have never taken place before and are quite spiritual in nature about love, souls, music, and teachings.) Have you run into other people who have experienced this type of communication or receptiveness?

I have a five-year-old daughter who never met my mother and was only eight months old when my father died, yet she speaks of them in her dreams, and they are similar to mine.

Notice how the account begins with the sentence, "With great trepidation I write, as I still find it hard to explain the DBV I had with my father back in 1997." Rob is not totally convinced I will accept his account, but as the sharing continues, he becomes more comfortable in opening up, and we learn several wonderful things about his journey. Not only has he encountered a DBV, he's also experienced numerous ADCs. Along with this, Rob shares that his young daughter is communicating with her deceased grandparents. Rob is beginning his spiritual journey. He is looking for validation of his STE encounters, but he is also in need of direction on where to turn to next. I was glad to be of service.

Rolling Up Our Shirt Sleeves

As we have seen, when traveling a path of spiritual enlightenment, life isn't always a smooth ride. If anything, many on such a road will be confronted with more than one spiritual lesson. Instead of sweeping these opportunities for growth under the rug, acting as if all is well, and life as it is is just fine, STE seekers often know intuitively that they must now roll up their shirtsleeves and get down to business. Unresolved relationship issues, addiction, dysfunction, old hurt, grief, and trauma can no longer be neglected. These once-hidden spiritual barriers now take on new meaning. With an STE encounter, this third group of roadblocks must also be addressed. Awareness of this often hits like a ton of bricks, and questions such as the following surface:

- If I'm to persue a spiritual life, how can I continue drinking excessively, popping pills, smoking pot daily, ignoring my health, or focusing all of my attention on work, fame, fortune, and material pursuits? My preoccupation with such things leaves little time for spiritual exploration. Where is the balance?
- I will never make peace with death and dying until I grieve the passing of my father, spouse, sibling, mother, friend, pet, or the childhood I lost to abuse, poverty, illness, addiction, divorce, war, or trauma. Hiding from it doesn't make it go away.
- One sexual affair after another isn't filling me up. I want true intimacy and connection with another human being. One-night stands and quick sexual interludes leave me feeling so empty. I want more.
- I hate myself. I hate my weight. My spirit is trapped behind walls of flesh, and I want out of this prison.

I want the freedom to explore my universe. My obsession with food is separating me from who I truly am.

- Why am I so unhappy? Why can't I feel true joy? Why was I born? What is my purpose?
- I want to feel and be a part of life. How can I connect with others who believe as I do? What should I do? I feel so alone, so alienated.
- I have an illness. How can I live with it? How can I improve the quality of my life, reclaim control from my illness, and live life to the fullest?
- Now that I've glimpsed a bigger world, seen the other side, and experienced powers greater than myself, how can I return to my life as it once was? How do I integrate my STEs into my daily living experience?

Often, an STE will pull the life issues we have avoided for years out of the darkest recesses of our mind. After my first STE, I was suddenly hit with strong feelings about unresolved incest, which had been a devastating part of my childhood. For years I had avoided addressing this painful part of my past, but an STE pushed me into finally healing this wound. My husband, Michael, a seasoned psychologist, was an adopted child. His first STE catapulted him into locating his biological parents. In doing this, he finally came to terms with being adopted. Shortly after an STE, unfinished business often ambushes the mind, assaulting the consciousness, demanding immediate attention. The unfinished must be finished in order to continue exploring a spiritual path.

The biggest mistake an STE-er can make is ignoring these issues. Not addressing our unfinished business will ultimately taint our STE. Once tainted, we will be at risk for missing its true message. How often I have seen STE-ers sidestep this important spiritual challenge and then misuse their encounter for fame and fortune. An STE does not make a person a spiritual guru, but there are those who have taken on this role. I have heard self-appointed STE gurus say in so many words, "Because I have had a near-death experience, after-death communication, Kundalini awakening, premonition, out-of-body experience, or departing vision, 'I' am much more spiritually evolved than the average person. So, 'I' will be your teacher. I will show 'You' the way to spiritual enlightenment."

If such individuals have not addressed their own unfinished business, they can be a danger to those who follow them. I have worked with many individuals who have been hurt by popular, self-appointed spiritual gurus. I can say, without hesitation, that these injuries have all been the direct byproduct of unfinished business, which contaminated an STE encounter. Many popular mediums, psychics, and NDE-ers, become lost in their own quest for power, and in this pursuit, their true purpose has evaporated. For this reason, know that if you are the seeker, you must do whatever is necessary to clear up any wreckage in your past. In attempting to heal these old wounds, you might need to find assistance from someone who understands both STEs and the need to resolve past life hurts. Friends and family might be able to provide you with initial support and a listening ear. But, in order to do the real work, you might need a bit more help. Finding assistance for this can be tricky. Here, we address our forth roadblock.

How to Find an "Ear"

One client of mine had a powerful after-death communication. Her deceased mother-in-law came to her one night. Standing there, at the foot of her bed, the spirit of this woman passed on to her daughter-in-law messages for the rest of the family. The ADC was an overwhelming spiritual encounter, and the thought of communicating this experience with other family members was terrifying. Long-standing rifts had kept her separated from close relatives. This woman needed validation for her ADC experience, along with assistance in resolving some of the resentments she had toward her family members. We spent several sessions together and addressed these past resentments. Once these were resolved, she was able to pass on to her family the message she had received from her mother-in-law.

With an STE, here-and-now life issues collide with spiritual questions, and help in sorting this out is often essential. How do we "go on" after having a powerful STE? Where can we turn to for support and guidance? How do we find the right person to talk to?

During times of uncertainty, those following a religious faith will turn to clergy for support. The thought is, "My minister, rabbi, or priest must understand spiritual experiences of this nature." Author, researcher, and Catholic priest Andrew Greeley has found that regardless of religious affiliation, belief in an afterlife appears to be on the rise, so it would seem natural that clergy would be the perfect choice.

ભ Belief in life after death has become more prevalent in the 1990s than it was in the 1970s, according to data from the General Social Survey. Year-to-year changes are significant. . . . Roughly 85 percent of Protestants believe in life after death. . . . The proportion of Catholics believing in the afterlife rose from 67 percent of the cohort (group) born 1900–09 to 85 percent of the cohort (group) born 1960–69. Among Jews, this belief increased from 17 percent of the 1900–09 cohort (group) to 74 percent of the 1960–69 cohort (group). Immigration is a key factor in the increase. Many Catholics and Jews arriving from Europe were, with the exception of Irish and Polish Catholics, hostile or indifferent to organized religion. Their children and grandchildren, socialized in the United States, have come to adopt the prevalent view that each person has a soul that lives on after the death of the body.[4]

The above statistics suggest faith in the soul's survival after death is on the increase, but does such a belief guarantee acceptance of STE encounters by clergy? Sadly, not always. After one of my first adult STEs, I thought to myself, "I'll visit with the rabbi who married me to my husband. Yeah! He will help me sort all of this out!" After explaining my STE encounter, this well-known rabbi looked at me as if I'd lost my marbles and said, "Have you seen a psychiatrist?" I replied, "No," and then proceeded to explain how the STE had brought my history of incest to the surface. After patting my knee, he asked me if I was on medication. I was stunned. Without going into further detail, let's just say seeking out help from this particular clergy person was a big, big mistake. I left his office in tears, feeling more confused than ever. Finding the right clergy person to talk to can take some research.

My good friend, Rabbi Jimmy Kessler, has shared with me his frustration regarding the lack of acceptance of STEs within religion. In his work as the rabbi of a fairly sizable congregation, STEs related to the dying experience are commonly encountered. Often, he and I will discuss such incidents over strong coffee. Though Rabbi Kessler is very open to STEs, he is the exception, not the norm. Here is what he had to say about the clergy's current lack of interest in the STE phenomenon.

∾ Historically—and even more so in recent history— the event of dying has been kept in hushed tones and only spoken of through funeral rites. Yet, at the same time, many occurrences surrounding death are rarely mentioned. Sometimes people present at a deathbed have seen or heard something leaving the body at the time of passing. Or, the dying individual has had visions of the other side and reported them to those at hand. Perhaps most interesting are experiences shared by the dying and those in their presence. That is, at the time of death, the dying and the people around them perceive the same, otherworldly phenomenon. . . . Humans commonly want permission to enter into new and uncharted areas. Where such permission is not available, investigation is often stifled. Perhaps the scarcity of communal knowledge of these stories stems from a lack of permission. Unfortunately, the religious institutions into whose context such stories are usually placed have not sanctioned such exposure.[5]

If a clergy person does not publicly "sanction" or acknowledge the STE phenomenon, but instead sees such experiences as signs of mental illness or a lack of faith, congregants will not openly share otherworldly encounters with this individual. Many times, clergy members must be hit over the head with an STE themselves before they can really "listen" to those they serve. Rabbi Kessler's son had a pre-birth experience. After looking at old photographs of his deceased grandparents in a picture album, the young two-year-old toddler announced to his father, "I know them. I met them before I came to live with you and Mommy." No one had ever told the child who his deceased grandparents were, nor had he ever seen pictures of them.

An STE experienced by a clergy person can forever change

how that religious leader addresses future STEs shared by those they serve.

A CLERGY STE

I was, and still am, very close to my mother. She left this world quickly (a heart aneurysm). At the exact moment of her departure, I awoke from a sound sleep at 1:35 A.M. At the time, I did not know why, but I was wide awake and strangely aware of everything around me, including sounds and sensations outside. I also felt refreshed, as though I had experienced a restful and full sleep.

There was no foreboding, fear, or anxiety, just rest and peace, and I wondered, "What's happening?"

For the next several days, really all month long, I had vivid dreams. In one dream, I saw my mother coming to reassure me that she was fine. At another time, while my father was sleeping, it seemed as though my mother was there. She was stroking his hair. Just as I saw this, she looked at me and then I fell back to sleep.

A week later, back in bed, I was fully awake when I felt a warm, solid hand pat and stroke my bare arm in the night. I was not fearful, but simply said, "I love you forever."

Then, in my mind, I suddenly saw angels lining up on both sides of my mother, and up into the night skies she went as she left my room. . . . Oh yes, by the way, I'm a minister.

This minister would be an ideal person with whom to discuss an STE, but where do we find such professionals? Possibly, your own clergy professional might be the perfect person with whom to share your account. Many religious leaders of congregations are also trained in family therapy or counseling. If you are comfortable with your clergy, meet with them and slowly introduce the topic of STEs *before* divulging your own experience. Questions such as the following can be a great way to break the ice and begin a conversation about the STE phenomenon with the clergy.

- What do you think about the NDEs reported in popular media? Have you read any literature on this?
- Do you believe our deceased relatives living in the afterlife watch over us? Can they communicate with us?
- Where do you think our souls go after we die? Do you believe it's possible for us to visit afterlife realms before we pass over?
- Some people believe they have had premonitions about future events. What do you think about that?
- Have you ever witnessed anything unusual at the bedside of a dying congregant?

If your clergy person appears interested, curious, or knowledgeable about these topics, share with him or her that you have had an unusual experience and would like to discuss it. Tell your clergy person up-front that you are a bit apprehensive about disclosing your account and that you fear you might not be believed. Ask your religious caretaker if he or she can keep an open mind. A healthy clergy person will listen without judgment, and if they themselves are lacking in the skill to assist you, they will refer you to literature or other professionals more suited to your needs.

As a mental-healthcare professional, I am often the first person with whom STE-ers discuss their encounters. Because I have both personally and professionally encountered numerous STEs, I'm very open to the experiences of others. Sadly, as with many clergy people, my professional peers aren't always accepting and supportive of STE-ers. Sue Darroch is one of the directors for a nonprofit organization that actively investigates STE claims. The organization, called Para-Researchers, is located in Ontario, Canada. Here is what she had to say about the need for professionals to "listen" with an open mind.

       It often breaks my heart when someone approaches me with an experience that would be considered "paranormal" in nature and relates how they have held it inside for decades because of a fear of ridicule, or perhaps worse, being branded as "crazy." The STE experiencer is in need of someone to listen to them with an open heart and mind, despite what the listener's current beliefs and religious/nonreligious persuasions might be. Certain types of STEs enable experiencers to cope with either their own mortality or loss. These STEs are seen as true blessings. This was true with my own experience and that of my dad, who had visions of his deceased mother shortly before he succumbed to cancer in July 1999. This phenomenon was an epiphany for me. Therefore, in my opinion, the most simplistic, and perhaps best, approach that professionals can take when dealing with those who relate STEs is to listen, learn from, and validate the experience. Allow for the experiencers to be able to express themselves freely within a compassionate and supportive environment. Let them know what they have observed is completely natural, positive, and has been shared by countless others throughout the world.[6]

If you, as an experiencer, decide to seek out the assistance of a psychologist or psychotherapist, here are a few questions you can ask over the telephone before making an appointment.

- Do you work with individuals who are spiritually struggling? Can you assist a person who has unresolved addictions, trauma, relationship issues, or grief?
- Will you refer me for medication if I begin expressing a lot of emotion, or will you assist me in processing and understanding my feelings?
- Have you ever investigated paranormal encounters, such as the near-death experience (NDE), after-death communication (ADC), and encounters with deceased relatives, precognition, or out-of-body experiences (OBE)?
- Do you see clients who have had these experiences, and if so, do you see such encounters as a sign of mental illness, hallucinations, or brain dysfunction?
- Have you read any of the research on near-death experiences, after-death communication, out-of-body experiences, premonitions, Kundalini awakenings, or departing visions? If so, what do you think about this?

With professional mental-healthcare workers you must be very up-front! Remember, you are the consumer, and the mental-healthcare professional will be providing you with a service. After interviewing a professional with the above questions, you will be able to determine quickly if this person will really be able to "hear" about your encounter. Along with this, you will recognize whether or not this individual can assist you in working through any unresolved life issues you might have.

Many of us also have long-standing relationships with our physicians. Some of us even consider the family doctor to be a friend. When confronted with a physical concern or even emotional distress, it is not uncommon to ring up this trusted professional for advice and assistance. Unfortunately, medical doctors are typically very scientifically minded, and for most,

STEs do not fall within the usual categories associated with medicine. I have had numerous debates with doctor friends about the STE phenomenon, and to date, I can report that most of my medical buddies have yet to investigate the scientific research available seriously. Generally speaking, with regard to this particular professional group, the well of open-mindedness continues to run pretty dry. But not all hope is lost. There are a few doctors out there who are cautiously open to learning about STE encounters. Some of these docs are even "closeted" experiencers themselves. Finding professionals such as these has personally proven to be very difficult, but perseverance has paid off. I have befriended several physicians who are very interested in learning more about the STE phenomenon. One of these unique professionals is Dr. Jeffery Long.

Dr. Long is a well-respected physician practicing the specialty of radiation oncology in Tacoma, Washington. Along with this, he is a researcher and a very interesting and courageous investigator. Dr. Long is not your typical doc. Aside from tending to patients, he researches near-death experiences, after-death communications, and pre-death visitations. Being very familiar with the STE, Dr. Long also serves as vice president on the Board of Directors of IANDS (International Association for Near-Death Studies).

Recently, he took on a large research project involving a survey of physicians' views and responses to patients who report NDEs. From Dr. Long's article, "Physician Views and Response to Patients' Near-Death Experience (NDE): A Survey," written in conjunction with colleague Judith Boss, Ph.D., we read:

    ᔕ In our NDE research, we have encountered a number of NDErs (person who experiences a near-death encounter) who describe unsatisfactory or unpleasant experiences when they tried to share their NDE with their physicians.[7]

Based on the results of his survey, Dr. Long theorizes that physicians who feel comfortable discussing NDEs with their patients might have had more exposure to the topic. Because of such exposure, they will be more accepting and better listeners. Out of 550 physicians surveyed, only six of the respondents felt "very comfortable" talking to patients about NDEs.

It is likely the six survey respondents who were very comfortable hearing about NDEs knew about and respected NDEs prior to hearing about their patients' NDEs. One respondent wrote, "I feel at ease discussing these experiences, and actually try to help the patient use the experience to help learn to experience greater peace in his or her life." If there were a higher level of comfort in both sharing and listening to NDEs, perhaps far more NDEs would be shared.[8]

Because otherworldly encounters are not common topics debated in medical schools, most physicians in general feel uneasy talking about STEs. This being the case, how do you know whether or not your physician will be able to hear you? The following questions will help:

- Do you know what a near-death experience is? Did you know there is an international scientific association comprised of physicians, psychologists, nurses, social workers, and other healthcare providers dedicated to understanding the near-death experience? This organization is called the International Association for Near-Death Studies.
- Do you see the near-death experience only as the byproduct of brain chemistry, or do you think there is more to it?

- Have year ever heard a dying patient talk about visions of deceased relatives before passing? If so, what did you think about that?
- Did you know that just before a loved one passes, family members sometimes have visions of deceased relatives, too? What do you think about that?
- If a patient were to come to you and share, "I had a dream about my recently deceased grandmother. It was so real. She was so happy, so animated, and she looked healthy and younger. She told me she was just fine and said I should not worry about her," would you immediately attribute this to stress, grief, or wishful thinking?

To be of utmost service, a helping professional does not have to be convinced that STEs are real, but they must have an open mind and be willing to hear experiences without passing judgment. As caregivers, they should be able to offer support, not negate the encounter. If you hear the following remarks from a mental-health caretaker, clergy, or medical professional, know this person most likely is not a good candidate for support.

- I believe these particular experiences are just a fabrication of the mind.
- You have been under tremendous stress, and I really do feel your mind has begun to play tricks on you.
- I recently read research that suggests deathbed visions and near-death experiences are just the byproduct of a dying brain.
- Meditation can bring on delusions and psychotic thinking that can be dangerous.
- Your dying loved one didn't really see, feel, or hear that. You are making too much out of it.

- Dreams are only related to everyday stresses. They don't really mean anything. It's just chemistry.
- Even though his illness wasn't related to brain function, and although he wasn't on medication, the vision he had about his deceased wife visiting him weeks before he passed was just a hallucination.
- You didn't have a premonition. That was just a coincidence.
- Our church doesn't acknowledge such things.
- Are you on medication? If not, you might need medication.
- These visions are not of God. They are evil.
- You have an overactive imagination. That's superstitious nonsense.
- You must be in serious grief over your loss or you are fearful of death. During these trying times, we all want to believe in such things. I strongly suspect you are suffering from a bout of wishful thinking.

Such remarks are usually based on personal experiences, religious belief systems, and life philosophy. They typically reflect very biased opinions, and though they might be true for a particular caregiver, such biases can quickly negate your STE, leaving you feeling unsupported. A listening ear with a compassionate nod is more healing than the above statements. A true, unprejudiced professional would never try to persuade a client, patient, or congregant to believe that an STE encounter was not real. As you the experiencer know, these otherworldly contacts are very real. When a healthcare provider projects their personal, spiritual, or religious beliefs on to you or condemns your STE in any way, understand that such an individual cannot be of assistance to you.

Just what does a healthy caretaker look like? An open-minded clergy, mental-healthcare provider, or physician will be interested in hearing your account. Such an individual will listen without interruption or judgment. They will want to know what impact this experience has had on you and how they can best serve your needs. Here are some ways to know that you have found a good healthcare provider, physician, or clergy member to listen to your experiences:

- The focus of discussion will rotate around you and your experience: "How has this affected you? Has the experience forced you to look at areas of your life you normally would have ignored?"
- Your emotions will be respected, and you will not be condemned for feeling elated, overwhelmed, joyous, confused, tearful, or lost: "It is normal to feel overwhelmed with emotion at a time like this."
- Support will be offered in the form of a compassionate nod, pat on the shoulder, or handholding. The caretaker might even say, "How can I help you get through this? Can I give you a hug?"
- Statements like, "That is amazing!" "How do you feel about this?" "What have you learned or discovered about yourself?" "Where would you like to go from here?" "What can I do to be of support?" and "Are you in need of resources, literature, or support groups that can assist you in understanding your experience?" show that the caretaker is there for you and not judgmental of your STE.

When you are able to find supportive listeners, you can then begin integrating your STEs into your everyday life. Proper counseling can provide you with the guidance you need to address those life issues the STE has uncovered. Healthy spiritual direction will enable you to begin seeking answers to the spiritual questions you have about your STE. After sharing your encounter with a supportive listener, you then might need more information, information related to what you have experienced. Once you find someone to listen to you, support you, and validate your feelings about your experience, you will have removed one more roadblock from your spiritual path. The next step involves learning all you can about your STE.

STE EDUCATION IS A POWERFUL TOOL

At the age of sixteen, when I had my first STE encounter, I had nowhere to turn. This made the experience painful and confusing. Not having a soul to talk to left me feeling very alone. Lacking validating information regarding the departing vision I had encountered at the time of my mother's death brought about great uncertainty, and a touch of fear. It took me a decade to find a listening ear, and it would be another five years before I picked up written literature describing deathbed visions in detail.

Dr. Mitchell shared how his STE in space left him feeling "scattered" and that it took him time to "pick up the pieces." In picking up the pieces, he created a worldwide organization, one that has validated hundreds of STE-ers. It is time for you to leave the pages of this book and journey forth, picking up your own pieces, as you establish a path that works for you. In defining your journey, know there are a number of institutions, groups, and other books dedicated to further exploring the human consciousness. Use them, and investigate what they have to offer. By bravely branching off into new territory, you will also connect with many fellow seekers. These like-minded travelers will be able to support you as you continue to unravel the mystery of yourself and the "worlds" around you.

Today, if I cross paths with the unseen world, I have lists of supports and friends to turn to. I would now like to share some of these resources with you. Use these spiritual "stop-offs" as you would a traveling map. While on vacation, I love pulling into little towns, taking short side trips. Sometimes these side trips turn out to be nothing more than temporary diversions. But, in many instances, I fall upon wonderful discoveries, which enrich my vacation. I look at my own spiritual travels in just this way. Understand that a true spiritual trek involves a lifelong quest for enlightenment, made fuller with numerous spiritual side trips and "stop-offs."

By mapping out and then beginning your own journey and traveling a spiritual path specifically suited to you, you will gain confidence with each stop you make. Be open to investigating the organizations I have listed in the "STE Educational Resource" section at the end of this book. Take the time to see what each group has to offer.

Finally, before ending our journey together, I would like to leave you with a parting gift. There is a saying taken from the work of William Shakespeare, which I live by, and it's simply stated: "To thine own self be true."

I would like to pass this on to you. Always be true to yourself, embrace your life experiences, and honor your feelings. In doing so, you can be assured that the spiritual road you travel will bless you with one awesome trip—one filled with incredible spiritual adventures and true moments of spiritual illumination.

chapter thirteen

STE Educational Resource Organizations

"Da is going to the sky, Mom!
The Angel told me so!"

—DBV experienced by Joshua Brandon, age three

Why STEs Are So Important

$\mathcal{I}$ have been investigating deathbed visions for a couple of decades. As I sat with my ailing mother-in-law for fourteen hours straight, I witnessed the most incredible deathbed visions. Who would have thought my skeptical mother-in-law would have been visited with such profound DBVs? My mother-in-law, Elizabeth Brandon, Ph.D., was not only a scientifically minded university professor, but she was the first woman chair of the French Linguistics Department at the University of Houston. Mom loved to debate world events and was a radical, no-nonsense feminist. Having lost her own mother to the Nazi gas camps, she had little interest in spiritual matters. Among her many students, the statement, "You must improve your mind," was considered a common "Madame Brandon quote." European born, schooled in Paris University and in Quebec, a published author, and researcher, Mom had no time for, as she called it, superstitious beliefs. Lets just say my mother-in-law was a pure intellectual.

Even Skeptics Can Experience STEs

On the day of her passing, Mom was initially very annoyed with her deathbed visions. In Polish, she told my husband's aunt, her sister, who had survived the Nazi death camp Auschwitz, "These visions are bothersome! Crazy!" My aunt then turned to my husband Michael and asked, "Why is she talking about visions?" I am so grateful both he and I were able to explain to her and the rest of the family what deathbed visions were. This eased their pain.

As the day wore on, it became obvious that Mom was talking to my father-in-law. She called to him using a word that means "monkey." This was her nickname for him. Pop had passed six years earlier. Along with this, she was also calling out to her mother, who had perished in a Nazi death camp. Time and time again, we as a family watched Mom reach out to embrace family invisible to us. When she couldn't hug them, she would drop her arms to her side and sigh with disappointment.

At this point, it is very important to note that Mom had not had any medication, nor was she suffering from brain or nervous-system disorders. My mother-in-law was very lucid, knew I was in the room, told her son, my husband, that she loved him, recognized her grandson, my oldest son Aaron, and also her nephew, her niece, and her niece's husband. She also told her sister she loved her.

During the early afternoon, things began to change. Mom

began arguing and telling her invisible visitors, "No! Not yet!" She wasn't ready to go. She began making hand movements, as if she were giving someone something. After a while and much conversation with her visitors in Polish, Yiddish, and French (her first languages), she then began grasping in front of her again, with arms outstretched, asking, "Help me. Please help me." She was asking her invisible visitors for help. Then, she would pause, and it was clear to us she was listening to her visitors. After listening, she would become annoyed again, let her arms fall, and say, "No! Not yet."

This went on for many hours. Eventually, I decided to get proactive, so I bent down, close to her ear, and calmly said, "Go with them. Relax. Don't be frightened. It's okay. You can stop fighting now." My husband also went to her, lovingly rubbed her tired arms, and said, "Mom, it's okay. We will be all right. You can go on. We love you." She listened to both of us.

Later on that evening, she was still arguing with her invisible visitors, but it was obvious to us that her fight was leaving her. Acceptance was slowly taking over. She now seemed desperate to be with them, but was not quite ready to give up the battle. The moon was rising high in the sky outside her window, and I was becoming concerned for my children, who were at home. One more time we heard Mom say, "No! Not yet." With this, my dog-tired husband and I looked at one another, and we could see the exasperation in each other's eyes. We knew without speaking that we needed to return home to our boys. I told Mom one more time, "Quit fighting. You are safe. It's all right. I love you." Michael also added, "I love you, Mom," and we then made our way home. After tucking the children into bed, Michael and I both fell into an exhausted sleep.

Several hours later, at 2:40 in the morning, I awoke with a "knowing" feeling that something wasn't right. Two blocks away, at that very same time, my mother-in-law finally let go, shed her tired body, and walked through the veil separating this life from the next. After crawling out from under stacks of pillows and the comfort of our bed, we called Mom's residence and learned she had indeed begun her journey to the afterlife at the exact moment I had awakened.

Awakening with such a knowing was nothing new for me. As I have already explained, when my own mother crossed over to the other side, I awoke at the exact moment of her passing, and her passage reached out and touched me. Other family friends were also touched. They, too, in separate locations, had been stirred from a deep sleep at the moment of her departure.

I never expected that my serious-minded mother-in-law would encounter DBVs. I'm grateful I was wrong. Watching her travel the road of angry defiance to one of acceptance and peace was absolutely amazing. I have reviewed close to 2,000 deathbed vision accounts, have experienced these myself, and have witnessed those of others, but none have been as profound for me as those of my mother-in-law's. Mom was not intimately familiar with my work. She had only a vague idea of my investigations. My last book, which discussed DBVs in depth, was definitely not tops on her reading list.

For those of you who are skeptical of what I have shared, know I recognize that not having had first-hand experience with matters of this nature makes the understanding of verbal accounts, after the fact, seem highly improbable. I do understand the thinking. But also understand that for the experiencer, such encounters create an intellectual shift. My perception of life, life after death, and the world as it is, as seen through the five senses, has changed dramatically over the years. Each new STE encounter creates one more shift, altering my perception just a bit more.

Over the decades, how I see life, reality, the world, and the universe at large has been drastically altered because of my first-hand encounters, and it differs radically from the non-experiencer. Does this make me more spiritual than the non-experiencer, more special, enlightened, or more aware? Not necessarily. My perception is just different.

My husband and children have also been exposed to numerous STEs. We talk openly with one another about these encounters. Because of this, we not only believe Mom's essence has moved on, but we see her DBVs as a blessing. We, as a family, are grateful to have been with her during her last moments. Because STEs are no longer foreign to us, we know Mom was blessed with a glimpse of heaven before she drew her final breath. What a gift she left us with. We love you, Mom.

I wrote the above account just days after my mother-in-law passed. My own STE encounters have not only changed the course of my life, but have also improved the quality of living for my family, by smoothing out the rough edges of life's difficulties. Today, we openly share these experiences, but there was a time when we felt such encounters kept us isolated.

After several STE encounters, I eventually climbed down off my own isolated emotional mountaintop and went looking for groups, organizations, and books that would:

1. Assist me in understanding that I was not alone in my experiences
2. Validate my STEs
3. Introduce me to other people who had such encounters
4. Provide me with methods for integrating these spiritual experiences into my life
5. Direct me toward those individuals who were scientifically investigating such encounters

Over the last twenty years, I'd say I've come up with a "top-notch" list, and now I'm going to pass this on to you. I strongly suggest you take the time to examine each of the resources below closely. While some of the following suggestions might seem alien and even uncomfortable, others will fit you like a glove. Go with your intuition, and trust your gut. If it feels right, it probably is just right for you. May your continued spiritual journey be filled with awe and adventure. If you would like to contact me, you can e-mail me at *glimpse ofheaven@msn.com* or send a letter to:

1010 2nd Street
League, Texas 77550

∼ STE-Related Organizations

The Academy of Religion and Psychical Research (ARPR)

The Academy of Religion and Psychical Research was formed in 1972. The organization is dedicated to encouraging dialogue, exchange of ideas, and cooperation between clergy, academics of religion and philosophy, scientists, researchers, and academics of all scientific and humanistic disciplines in the fields of psychical research. Near-death experiences, after-death communications, Kundalini awakenings, religious and paranormal encounters, meditation, altered states of consciousness, and communication with the deceased are just a few of the topics regularly investigated by the ARPR. Members of this group use the ARPR as a forum to share research findings and to present new theories as they relate to psychical research. Historical investigations are also examined. The Academy sponsors lectures and conferences for the purpose of presenting research and publishes a journal.

> *The Academy of Religion and Psychical Research*
> P.O. Box 614
> Bloomfield, Connecticut 06002-0614
> Telephone: (860) 242-4593
> *www.lightlink.com/arpr*

After Death Communication Research Foundation (ADCRF)

Jeffery Long, M.D., started the After Death Communication Research Foundation (ADCRF) several years ago. Dr. Long is a well-respected physician in Tacoma, Washington, who specializes in radiation oncology. Along with this, he is a well-respected ADC researcher, dedicated to bringing understanding of such encounters to the medical field.

> *After Death Communication Research Foundation*
> P.O. Box 23367
> Federal Way, Washington 98093
> Fax: (253) 568-7778
> *www.adcrf.org*

The American Society for Psychical Research (ASPR)

Founded in 1885 by a group of interested researchers, including the Harvard psychologist William James, the ASPR is the oldest psychical research organization in the United States. Made up of an international membership, the ASPR has an incredible library containing manuscripts, case studies, investigations, and rare books, dating back to the 1700s. The ASPR continues to be in the forefront of scientific investigation into unexplained psychic phenomenon and human consciousness, providing education and information to professionals and laypeople alike. Located in New York City, this organization houses not only offices, but also laboratories for research. The well-respected *ASPR Journal* was first published in 1907 and continues to the present date.

> *American Society for Psychical Research*
> 5 West 73rd Street
> New York, New York 10023
> Telephone: (212) 799-5050
> Fax: (212) 496-2497
> *www.aspr.com*

The Association for Research and Enlightenment (ARE)

Founded by psychic Edgar Cayce in 1931, the ARE continues to be dedicated to providing spiritually centered education to the public. Based on Cayce's forty-three years of work as a popular psychic, topics of investigation include dreams, intuition, personal spirituality and health. The ARE provides its membership with numerous programs, lectures, services, and activities. Though Edgar Cayce died in 1945, his accurate psychic readings, discussed in more than 300 written works, continue to be examined by researchers.

> *The Association for Research and Enlightenment*
> 215 67th Street
> Virginia Beach, Virginia 23451
> Telephone: (757) 428-3588 or (800) 333-4499
> *www.are-cayce.com*

Institute of Noetic Sciences (IONS)

In 1971, several like-minded thinkers, interested in understanding and researching human potential and consciousness,
originally founded this wonderful international organization.
Since its beginnings, researchers associated with IONS have
been scientifically rigorous in their investigations. Topics
including medicine and consciousness, altered states of consciousness, near-death experiences, and physics are just a few of
the subjects studied in depth by IONS researchers. One of the
founding members, real-life, moon-walking Apollo 14 astronaut,
engineer, and scientist, Dr. Edgar Mitchell, continues to be very
involved with the institute. Information about conferences,
educational seminars, research articles, and journals is available
through the institute.

> *Institute of Noetic Sciences*
> 101 San Antonio Road
> Petaluma, California 94952
> Telephone: (707) 775-3500
> Fax: (707) 781-7420
> *www.noetic.org*

International Association for Near-Death Studies (IANDS)

In the 1970s, Dr. Raymond Moody and Dr. Elisabeth Kubler-
Ross brought the near-death experience to public light. Dr.
Bruce Greyson, Dr. Kenneth Ring, Dr. Michael Sabom, and
others, such as researcher John White, followed up Moody and
Kubler-Ross's research with investigations of their own. The
combined efforts of these researchers is at the foundation of
IANDS. Today, IANDS serves as an educational resource for
NDE-ers, researchers, healthcare professionals, and the general

public. Dedicated to further investigating near-death encounters and similar experiences, IANDS supplies information on
NDE support groups, literature, and conference locations.
IANDS's professional journal presents the most current
research and thought in NDE investigation.

International Association for Near-Death Studies
P.O. Box 502
East Windsor Hill, Connecticut 06028-0502
Telephone: (860) 644-5216 (Voice)
Fax: (860) 644-5759
www.iands.org

The Kundalini Research Network (KRN)

The KRN consists of researchers, scholars, healthcare professionals, and individuals interested in the Kundalini experience.
When one experiences a sudden surge of physical, emotional, or
psychic power as a result of yoga, meditation, or other forms of
consciousness transformation, these byproducts are often pathol-
ogized by healthcare professionals. This intense experience of
power, also known as the Kundalini encounter, is a type of STE
that continues to be misunderstood by physicians, mental healthcare workers, and the public at large. The goal of the KRN is to
provide accurate information about the Kundalini experience to
experiencers, healthcare professionals, and other researchers.

Kundalini Research Network
c/o Lawrence Edwards, Ph.D.
66 Main Street
Bedford Hills, New York 10507
Telephone: (914) 241-8510
www.kundalininet.org

The Monroe Institute—OBE Research

Forty years ago, out-of-body investigator Robert Monroe founded the Monroe Institute. His initial interest in human consciousness propelled him into setting up a small research center in New York in 1956. The intent of his investigation was to examine learning during sleep. In 1958, the OBE emerged (state of being where consciousness and the physical body are separate). Monroe's research then took him and his team in a totally different direction. Since that time, the institute has been dedicated to exploring different aspects of human consciousness, and thousands of people have benefited from the group's lectures, workshops, and on-site educational programs.

> *The Monroe Institute*
> 62 Roberts Mountain Road
> Faber, Virginia 22938-2317
> Telephone: (804) 361-1252
> Fax: (434) 361-1237
> *www.monroe-inst.com*

The Parapsychology Foundation

This organization is dedicated specifically to researching psychic encounters. Founded approximately fifty years ago, the Parapsychology group provides a worldwide forum for investigators to share their research with one another and the public. Delving into the areas of precognition, near-death experiences, after-death communications, meditative-related experiences, mediumship, and other psychic phenomena, this group continues to be a leader in the realm of psychic research, by providing grants for research projects, pamphlets for public use, conferences, and lecture series. Along with these things, the foundation produces the *International Journal of Parapsychology*.

Parapsychology Foundation, Inc.
228 East 71st Street
New York, New York 10021
Telephone: 212-628-1550
Fax: 212-628-1559
www.parapsychology.org

The Society for Psychical Research (SPR)

Dedicated to researching spirit encounters, hypnosis, clairvoyance, levitation, deathbed visions, trance states, telepathy, precognition, and related psychic experiences, the SPR is one of the oldest organizations of its type. Sir William Barrett and Edmund Dawson Rogers originally founded the group. Its initial purpose was for investigating true mediums and weeding out frauds. During the early years, this organization was comprised of members such as Carl Jung and Sigmund Freud. The American psychologist William James was so impressed with the SPR that he later formed a sister organization in the States in 1884. Today, the SPR has an extensive library composed of investigation into psychic phenomenon, and the organization continues its work, providing lecture series, literature, and a forum for research.

The Society for Psychical Research
49 Marloes Road
Kensington, London W8 6LA
Telephone and fax: (020) 7937-8984
www.spr.ac.uk

∾ STE Web Sites in Cyberspace

Afterlife Communication

After-Death Communication Site/*Hello From Heaven*
www.after-death.com

Prayer Wave/ADC Support
www.geocities.com/adcfriends

Afterlife Research

The Afterlife Experiments: Breakthrough Scientific Evidence of Life After Death
by Gary Schwartz, Ph.D.
www.openmindsciences.com

The International Survivalist Society—Disseminating the Scientific Case for Survival After Death on a Global Level
www.survivalafterdeath.org/home.htm

A Lawyer Presents the Case for the Afterlife—Irrefutable Objective Evidence
by Victor Zammit
www.victorzammit.com

Animals and the Afterlife

Animal Afterlife Homepage
Animals and the Afterlife—True Stories of Our Best Friends' Journey Beyond Death
by Kim Sheridan
www.animalsandtheafterlife.com

Auras and the Human Energy Field

Kirlian Research
www.crystalinks.com/kirlian_photography.html

Dream Research

Dream Research/Dale Graff on Dreams and Their Psychic Nature
www.chesapeake.net/~baygraff/dreams.htm

Deathbed or Parting Visions

Deathbed Vision Investigations/Dr. Carla Wills-Brandon, Ph.D.
www.carla.wills.brandon.net

Parting Visions of the Dying/Dr. Melvin Morse, M.D.
www.melvinmorse.com

Grief Support

Bereaved Parents of the USA   GriefNet
www.bereavedparentsusa.org   *http://griefnet.org*

Kundalini Awakening Information

Kundalini Resource Center
http://hmt.com/kundalini

Meditation Research

Meditation Research Files
www.wisespirit.com/medresrch.htm

Near-Death Experiences

Near-Death Experiences and the Afterlife Resource Page
www.near-death.com

Near-Death Researcher Dr. Raymond Moody, M.D.
www.psychomanteum.com/books/drmoody.htm

Out-of-Body Research

Out-of-Body Research with Jeffery Long, M.D.
www.oberf.org

Premonitions

Central Premonitions Registry
www.mainportals.com/precog.shtml

Researched Mediums

George Anderson
www.georgeanderson.com

James Van Praagh
www.vanpraagh.com

John Edward
www.johnedward.net

Ingo Swann
www.biomindsuperpowers.com

Uri Geller
www.urigeller.com

∾ Resources for Psychotherapy, Self-Help Groups, and Addiction Recovery

Alcoholics Anonymous
www.alcoholics-anonymous.org

American Hospice Foundation
www.americanhospice.org

Family Service and Learning Centers
www.familycenteronline.org

Online Recovery 12-Step Self-Help and Support Groups
www.onlinerecovery.org/12

United Way of America Agencies
www.unitedway.org

Suggested Reading List

After-Death Communication

Guggenheim, B. and Guggenheim, J. *Hello From Heaven.* (New York: Bantam Books, 1996)

Moody, R. A. and Perry, P. *Reunions: Visionary Encounters with Departed Loved Ones.* (New York: Villard Books, 1994)

Van Praagh, J. *Talking to Heaven.* (New York: Dutton, 1997)

Deathbed or Departing Visions of the Dying

Barrett, W. *Death-Bed Visions.* (London: Methuen, 1926)

Morse, M. *Parting Visions: Uses and Meanings of Pre-Death, Psychical and Spiritual Experiences.* (New York: Villard Books, 1994)

Osis, K. and Haraldsson, E. *At the Hour of Death.* (New York: Avon Books, 1977)

Wills-Brandon, C. *One Last Hug Before I Go: The Mystery and Meaning of Deathbed Visions.* (Deerfield Beach, FL: HCI Inc., 2000)

Wooten-Green, R. *When the Dying Speak: How to Listen to and Learn from Those Facing Death.* (Chicago, IL: Loyola Press, 2001)

Near-Death Experiences

Carson, C. (Ed.) *When Ego Dies: A Compilation of Near-Death and Mystical Conversion Experiences.* Houston, TX: Emerald Ink Publ., 1996)

Harpur, T. *Life After Death.* (Toronto, Ontario: McClelland & Stewart, 1992)

Morse, M. with Perry, P. *Closer to the Light: Learning from Children's Near-Death Experiences.* (New York: Villard Books, 1990)

Steiger, B. and Steiger, S. H. *Children of the Light: The Startling and Inspiring Truth About Children's Near-Death Experiences and How They Illuminate the Beyond.* (New York: Signet, 1995)

Peak Meditation Experiences

Greenwell, B. *Energies of Transformation: A Guide to the Kundalini Process.* (Cupertino, CA: Shakti River Press, 1995)

Krishna, G. *The Awakening of Kundalini.* (Ontario, Canada: Institute for Consciousness Research, 1989)

Mitchell, E., and Williams, D. *The Way of the Explorer: An Apollo Astronaut's Journey Through the Material and the Mystical Worlds.* (Itasca, IL: Putnam Publishing, 1996)

Steiger, B. and Steiger, S. H. *Touched by Heaven's Light.* (New York: Signet/Penguin Putnam, 1999)

Wesselman, H. B., and Wesselman, H. *Spiritwalker: Messages From the Future.* (New York: Bantam Books, 1996)

Premonitions or Precognition

Altea, R. *The Eagle and the Rose: A Remarkable True Story.* (Warner Books, London, 1996)

Robinson, C. with Boot, A. *Dream Detective.* (Warner Books, London, 1996)

Rogers, L. W. *Dreams and Premonitions.* (Kessinger Publishing Company, 1942)

Smith, S., Schwartz, G., and Russek, L. *The Afterlife Codes: Searching for Evidence of the Survival of the Soul.* (Charlottesville, VA: Hampton Roads, 2000)

Out-of-Body Experiences

Monroe, R. A. *Ultimate Journey.* (New York: Doubleday, 1994)

Muldoon, S., and Carrington, H. *The Phenomenon of Astral Projection.* (New York: Samuel Weiser, Inc., 1970)

Taylor, A. *Soul Traveler: A Guide to Out-of-Body Experiences and the Wonders Beyond.* (New York: New American Library Trade, 2000)

Thompson Smith, A. and Swan, I. *Remote Perceptions: Out-of-Body Experiences, Remote Viewing and Other Normal Abilities.* (Charlottesville, VA: Hampton Roads, 1998)

STE Research

Korotkov, K. *Light After Life: A Scientific Journey into the Spiritual World.* (Fair Lawn, NJ: Backbone Publishing Company, 1998)

Moody, R. A., Jr. *Life After Life: The Investigation of a Phenomenon— Survival of Bodily Death.* (St. Simon Island, GA: Mockingbird Books, 1975)

Morse, D. *Searching for Eternity: A Scientist's Spiritual Journey to*

Overcome Death Anxiety. (Memphis, TN: Eagle Wing Books, Inc., 2000)

Ring, K. *Life at Death: A Scientific Investigation of the Near-Death Experience.* (New York: Coward, McCann & Geoghegan, 1980)

Schwartz, G. *The Afterlife Experiments: Breakthrough Scientific Evidence of Life After Death.* (New York: Pocket Books, 2002)

Zammit, V. *A Lawyer Presents a Case for the Afterlife* (3rd Edition). (Sydney, Australia: Ganmell Pty, Ltd., 2002)

Endnotes

Chapter 2

1. Munn, M. *X-Rated: The Paranormal Experiences of the Movie Star Greats*. (London: Robson Books, 1996), p. 70.
2. Harris, W. T., Editor in Chief. *Webster's New International Dictionary of the English Language*. (Springfield, MA: G & C Merrium Company, 1926), p. 1,619.
3. Munn, M. *X-Rated: The Paranormal Experiences of the Movie Star Greats*. (London: Robson Books, 1996), p. 63.
4. Dennet, P. E. "Premonitions of Disaster—Do Tragic Events Cast Shadows Before Them?" *Atlantis Rising*, Issue 18, Winter 1999. *www.atlantisrising.com/issue18/18premonitions.html*
5. Burman, A. "Premonitions of Death for *Titanic* Passengers," *Northampton Chronicle and Echo*, 14 February 1998. *http://homepage.ntlworld.com/ashleyrunt/premo.htm*
6. Ibid.
7. Dennet, P. E. "Premonitions of Disaster—Do Tragic Events Cast Shadows Before Them?" *Atlantis Rising*, Issue 18, Winter 1999. *www.atlantisrising.com/issue18/18premonitions.html*
8. Carrington, H. *Psychical Phenomena and the War*. (New York: American Universities Publishing Company, 1920), p. 158–59.
9. Dennet, P. E. "Premonitions of Disaster—Do Tragic Events Cast Shadows Before Them?" *Atlantis Rising*, Issue 18, Winter 1999. *www.atlantisrising.com/issue18/18premonitions.html*

10. Munn, M. *X-Rated: The Paranormal Experiences of the Movie Star Greats.* (London: Robson Books, 1996), p. 65.

11. Ibid, p. 69.

12. Morse, D. *Searching for Eternity: A Scientist's Spiritual Journey to Overcome Death Anxiety.* (Memphis, TN: Eagle Wing Books Inc., 2000), p. 65–66.

13. *TIME.* "Dreaming of Baby" by Lisa McLaughlin. 26 June 2000, p. 82.

Chapter 3

1. Levine, S. *Healing into Life and Death.* (New York: Doubleday Publishing, 1987). *www.commercemarketplace.com/home/fawwcf/healingpassage.html*

2. Morse, M. with Perry, P. *Parting Visions: Uses and Meanings of Pre-Death, Psychic and Spiritual Experiences.* (New York: Villard Books, 1994), p. 15.

3. Raphael, S. P. *Jewish Views of the Afterlife.* (London: Jason Aronson, 1996), p. 340.

4. Wills-Brandon, C. *One Last Hug Before I Go: The Mystery and Meaning of Death-Bed Visions.* (Deerfield Beach, FL: HCI Inc., 2000), p. 31–32.

5. Osis, K. and Erlendur, H. *At the Hour of Death.* (New York: Avon Books, 1977).

6. Barrett, W. *Death Bed Visions: The Psychical Experiences of the Dying.* (London: Psychic Press, 1926; Reprint. Northamptonshire, England: Aquarian Press, 1986), p. 18–19.

7. Miller, R. D. *You DO Take It with You.* (New York: Citadel Press, 1955).

8. Barrett, W. *Death Bed Visions: The Psychical Experiences of the Dying.* Introduction by Colin Wilson. (Wellingborough, Northamptonshire, England: The Aquarian Press, 1986), p. 19–20.

9. Cunningham, J. "Ancient Egyptian Mythology: A Model for Consciousness," *The Journal of Regression Therapy.* Volume XII, No. 1, December 1998, p. 86–96.

10. Carrington, H. *Psychical Phenomena and the War.* (New York: American Universities Publishing Company, 1920), p. 182–83.

Chapter 4

1. Morse, D. *Searching for Eternity: A Scientist's Spiritual Journey to Overcome Death Anxiety.* (Memphis, TN: Eagle Wing Books, 2000), p. 92.

2. Barrett, W. *Death Bed Visions: The Psychic Experiences of the Dying.* (Willingborough, Northhamptonshire, England: Aquarian Press, 1986, original 1926), p. 59.

3. Wills-Brandon, C. *One Last Hug Before I Go: The Mystery and Meaning of Deathbed Visions.* (Deerfield Beach, FL: HCI Inc., 2000), p. 13–14.

4. Morse, M. with Perry, P. *Parting Visions: Uses and Meanings of Pre-Death, Psychic, and Spiritual Experiences.* (New York: Villard Books, 1994), p. 19.

5. Barrett, W. *Death-bed Visions: The Psychic Experiences of the Dying.* (Willingborough, Northhamptonshire, England: Aquarian Press, 1986, original 1926), p. 61–63.

Chapter 5

1. Munn, M. *X-Rated: The Paranormal Experiences of the Movie Star Greats.* (London: Robson Books, 1996), p. 12.

2. Morse, D. *Searching for Eternity: A Scientist's Spiritual Journey to Overcome Death Anxiety.* (Memphis, TN: Eagle Wing Books, 2000), p. 93.

3. Ibid, p. 92.
4. Siciliano, H. "True Liberation," *Vital Signs*, Volume 16, Number 3, 1997, p. 9.
5. Bingham, Bill, Ed. Foreword D. K. Corcoran. *When Ego Dies: A Compilation of Near-Death and Mystical Conversion Experiences.* (Houston, TX: Emerald Ink Publishing, 1996), p. 129–31.
6. Seelig, M. "Near-Death Experiences and the Kundalini Phenomenon," *Vital Signs*, Volume 16, Number 3, 1998, p. 4–6.

Chapter 6

1. Morse, D. *Searching for Eternity: A Scientist's Spiritual Journey to Overcome Death Anxiety.* (Memphis, TN: Eagle Wing Books Inc., 2000), p. 99.
2. Myers, A. "Cats Who Fly," excerpted from *Communicating with Animals: The Spiritual Connection Between People and Animals.* (New York: McGraw Hill/Contemporary Books, 1997).
www.globalpsychics.com/lp/AnimalsTalk/Stories/Catsfly.htm
3. Price, J. *The Other Side of Death.* (New York: Ballantine/Fawcett Books, 1996). *www.near-death.com/experiences/Price01.html*
4. Guiley, R. E. *Harper's Encyclopedia of Mystical and Paranormal Experiences.* (Edison, NJ: Castle Books, 1991), p. 245.
5. Sheldrake, R. *Dogs That Know When Their Owners Are Coming Home—And Other Unexplained Powers of Animals.* (New York: Three Rivers Press, 2000).

Chapter 7

1. Nicholson, H. *The Knights Templar: A New History*. (United Kingdom: Sutton Publishing, 2001).
2. Temple Church: Pitkins Guides, Healey House, Dene Road, Andover, Hampshire, SP10 2AA, UK.
3. Wills-Brandon, C. *Learning to Say No: Establishing Healthy Boundaries*. (Deerfield Beach, FL: HCI Inc., 1990).

Chapter 8

1. Stern, Chaim, Ed. *Gates of Repentance: The New Union Prayer Book for the Day of Awe*. (New York: Central Conference of American Rabbis, 1978), p. 494.
2. "Controlled Experiment of Precognitive Dream Intelligence in a Highly Skilled Subject," *The Journal for Psychical Research*, p. 13.
3. Guiley, R. E. *Harper's Encyclopedia of Mystical and Paranormal Experiences*. (Edison, NJ: Castle Books, 1991), p. 463.

Chapter 9

1. Wedick, H. E. *Dictionary of Magic*. (New York: Philosophical Library, 1956), p. 28.
2. Toffelmier, G., and Luomala, K. "Dreams and Dream Interpretation of the Diegueno Indians of Southern California," *The Psychoanalytic Quarterly*. 5:1936, p. 195–225.
3. Wedick, H. E. *Dictionary of Magic*. (New York: Philosophical Library, 1956), p. 28.
4. The Jewish Publication Society of America. *The Holy Scriptures, New Edition*. (Philadelphia: Second Impression, 1961), p. 1,066.

5. Ibid, p. 451.
6. Ibid, p. 56.
7. Freud, S. Translated by Brill, A. A. *The Interpretation of Dreams (Third Edition)*, 1911, first page of Chapter 7, Books on Psych Web *www.psychwww.com/books/index.htm*.
8. Ibid.
9. Tart, C. "From Spontaneous Event to Lucidity: A Review of Attempts to Consciously Control Nocturnal Dreaming." Wolman, B., Ullman, M. and Webb, W. (Eds.), *Handbook of Dreams: Research, Theories and Applications*. (New York: Van Nostrand Reinhold, 1979), p. 255.

Chapter 10

1. Munn, M. *X-Rated: The Paranormal Experiences of the Movie Star Greats*. (London: Robson Books, 1996), p. 74.
2. Sperling, H. and Simon, M. Translators, *The Zohar 5 vols*. (London: Soncino Press, 1933, 1956).
3. Buber, M. *Tales of the Hasidim, Vol. 2, The Later Masters*. (New York: Schocken Books, 1977), p. 95.
4. Raphael, S. P. *Jewish Views of the Afterlife*. (Northvale, NJ: Jason Aronson, Inc, 1996), p. 290.
5. Butler, A. *The Lives of the Fathers, Martyrs and Other Principal Saints, Volume 1*. (London: Virtue and Company, Ltd., 1954).
6. Gandhi, Mohandas Karamchand, Microsoft® Encarta® Online Encyclopedia 2001. *http://encarta.msn.com* © 1997–2000 Microsoft Corporation.
7. James, Karen. *From Mohandas to Mahatma: The Spiritual Metamorphosis of Gandhi*. Essays in History, Volume 28. (Virginia: The Corcoran Department of History at the University of Virginia, 1984), p. 5.
8. Ibid.

9. Lewis, J. R. and Steiner, R. *Encyclopedia of Afterlife Beliefs and Phenomenon.* (Farmington Hills, MI: The Gale Group, 1994).

10. Albom, M. *Tuesdays with Morrie.* (New York: Double Day Publishing, 1997).

11. Kenny L. "Jack Lemmon, Hank Azaria Probe Meaning of Life in Heartfelt 'Tuesdays with Morrie,'" *The Orange County Register*: Distributed by the *Associated Press* (AP) 3 December 1999.

Chapter 11

1. Wooten-Green, R. *When the Dying Speak: How to Listen to and Learn from Those Facing Death.* (Chicago: Loyola Press, 2001), p. 187.

2. Morse, M. and Perry, P. *Parting Visions, Uses, and Meanings of Pre-death, Psychic, and Spiritual Experiences.* (New York: Villard Books, 1994), p. 71.

Chapter 12

1. Gallup Poll Analyses. "Americans' Belief in Psychic and Paranormal Phenomena," Poll Analyses 8 June 2001. List by Frank Newport and Maura Strausberg. (Princeton, NJ: Gallup News Service). *www.gallup.com/search/results.asp*

2. Mitchell, E. with Williams, D. *The Way of the Explorer: An Apollo Astronaut's Journey Through the Material and Mystical Worlds, Second Edition.* (Buenos Aires, Argentina: Richter Artes Graficas, 2001), p. 51.

3. Lommel, P., Wees, R., Meyers, V., and Elfferich, I. "Near-Death Experiences in Survivors of Cardiac Arrest: A Prospective

Study in the Netherlands," *The Lancet*, 15 December 2001, Volume 358, Issue 9,298, p. 2,010–2,039.

4. Mitchell, E. with Williams, D. *The Way of the Explorer: An Apollo Astronaut's Journey Through the Material and Mystical Worlds, Second Edition.* (Buenos Aires, Argentina: Richter Artes Graficas, 2001), p. 3–5.

5. Greeley, A. and Hout, M. (Working Paper). "Pie in the Sky While You're Alive: Americans' Belief in Life After Death." Supply-side Religion Berkeley, CA. Berkeley Survey Research Center, October 1998.

6. Sarah Darroch, director. Para-Researchers of Ontario, Canada. *www.pararesearchers.org*

7. Wills-Brandon, C. *One Last Hug Before I Go: The Mystery and Meaning of Deathbed Visions.* (Deerfield Beach, FL: HCI Inc., 2000), p. xiii–xv.

8. Long, J. and Boss, J. *Physician Views and Response to Patients' Near-Death Experience (NDE): A Survey 1999.*